JUMPSTART!
LITERACY

GAMES AND ACTIVITIES FOR AGES 7 – 14

Pie Corbett

 David Fulton Publishers

This edition reprinted 2006 by Routledge
2 Park Square, Milton Park, Abingdon, Oxon, OX14 4RN
Simultaneously published in the USA and Canada
By Routledge
270 Madison Avenue, New York, NY 10016

First published in Great Britain by David Fulton Publishers 2004
Reprinted 2004 (three times), 2005, 2006 (twice), 2007

10 9

British Library Cataloguing in Publication Data
A catalogue record for this book is available from the British Library.

ISBN 1 84312 102 6

Typeset by Mark Heslington, Scarborough, North Yorkshire
Cover Design by Martin Cater
Printed and bound in Great Britain

Contents

Acknowledgements

Many thanks to Linda Newbery, Philip Gross, James Carter and Katherine Gallagher for specific writing games. I am also immensely grateful to all the other writers, teachers and children who have shared their ideas with me over the years.

A different version of the anagrams in Chapter 2 (pp. 30–31) appeared in *Wordspinning*, edited by John Foster (Oxford University Press 2003).

'The Wolf's wife speaks' (p. 123) and 'The poem imagines it is a horror film' (p. 109) appeared in *Poems Out Loud*, selected by Brian Moses (Hodder Wayland 2003). You can hear Pie reading the poems on the CD accompanying that book.

'Six things found in an elf's backpack' (p. 112) first appeared in *The Snake's Pyjamas*, edited by Pie Corbett and Valerie Bloom (Ginn 2003).

'Sought it out!' (p. 14) first appeared in *Poems for Year 4*, chosen by Pie Corbett (Macmillan Children's Books 2002).

Introduction

Jumpstart! provides a series of quick-fire language games that can be used in a variety of ways to 'jumpstart' creative literacy.

HOW CAN THE GAMES BE USED?

- **As starters:** most of the activities can be used to start a literacy session off. The advantage of using a 'starter' is that everyone is involved from the beginning. These activities are also useful for 'warming up' the brain and are an excellent way to help tune participants' minds into thinking and concentrating. The ideas in the final chapter are generic and can be used in most subjects as strategies for learning.
- **As bridgers:** sometimes a 'jumpstart' activity can help to provide stimulus during the course of a lesson, possibly prior to leading into a more in-depth activity.
- **As finishers:** most of the activities could just as easily be used to end a session during the plenary. These might be used to consolidate what has been learned during the lesson, or to tantalise the class with a taste of what is to come next!
- **At odd moments:** the quick-fire nature of these activities means that nearly all of them are perfect for slotting in when you happen to have a spare five minutes on your hands.

WHY USE THE ACTIVITIES?

The activities presented in this book can be used to:

- jumpstart a creative mood
- stimulate creative thinking
- strengthen the imagination
- have fun with language, creativity and thinking
- introduce or revisit a topic
- consolidate learning
- provide practice – to secure confidence
- improve – taking a topic one step further
- grab attention – focusing children at the start/ during/end of a session
- assess understanding (using mini-whiteboards is a simple way of helping the teacher see whether most of the class has grabbed an idea).

LITTLE AND OFTEN

Some children need to revisit what has been taught on many occasions before they grasp or remember an idea. Spelling and sentence writing are often improved by regular short-burst activities.

ADAPTING THE GAMES

While I have often provided examples, model sentences or word lists, these should be adapted according to the needs of the class. For instance, many of the spelling games require you to select words/patterns that you are trying to teach or that a class keep finding difficult. When playing sentence games you may wish to invent sentences that relate to the type of text that you are teaching, or to use sentence structures that will help the children develop as writers.

WHAT YOU WILL NEED

All that you need to play many of these games is a class set of mini-whiteboards and some sort of whole-class board. Where other materials are required, these have been indicated clearly at the start of an activity.

TIPS ON HOW TO APPROACH 'JUMPSTARTING'

Here is a list of advice from teachers who use this approach regularly in their teaching:

- Keep the pace going – most responses need only take 10–15 seconds.
- A 'jumpstart' session might take 5–15 minutes.
- Challenge the class – for instance, ask those children who keep writing short sentences to extend them, perhaps by using the word 'because'.
- If using mini-whiteboards, don't wait for the last person to finish or you will be setting the pace by the slowest child.
- Many of the activities lend themselves to using mini-whiteboards, but could also be played with oral responses.
- If children struggle, model a few responses yourself to show them how to complete the activity, then complete a few on a whole-class board with the children helping.
- Move strugglers close to you so that you can see what they are doing – often they just need encouragement or a prompt.
- Activities may be played in pairs or individually. If in pairs, children should take turns (i.e. the person not holding the board could check what the other one has written).

- For some activities adopt a 'think – pair – share' approach: 'think' (about the task), 'pair' (discuss in pairs), 'share' (be ready to share your response with the class).

FINALLY – KEEP IT MULTI-SENSORY

Many of the 'jumpstarts' in this book are about developing thinking in a lively and creative way. The imagination can be strengthened, and some of these exercises will help children develop the ability to think creatively. The activities have been designed to help you use a balance of multi-sensory approaches in order to appeal to different learning styles:

- **Visual** – using objects, pictures and images
- **Auditory** – using sounds, voices, music
- **Cognitive** – using mnemonics, memory tricks, rules
- **Kinaesthetic** – using actions, drama, movement.

Symbols for each of these learning styles have been included at the start of each game, to show which of them are being targeted during the course of an activity.

| Visual | Auditory | Cognitive | Kinaesthetic |

The most important thing of all is to ensure that everyone has fun in the process!

Pie Corbett
August 2003

CHAPTER 1
Jumpstarting spelling

The activities in this chapter focus on improving spelling through a multi-sensory approach. Many children find spelling difficult and this hinders their ability to compose fluently. Spelling needs to be automatic (even if it is not a hundred per cent accurate!). A ten-minute daily session of whole-class spelling games can be a more effective way of helping children remember patterns than relying on a once-a-week spelling bash. Within a ten-minute session you could cover two or three games. Focus on words and patterns that they need, find difficult, or are the ongoing objective from your scheme.

RIGHT FROM WRONG

This game is quick and easy. It helps children look carefully at a spelling and try to decide whether or not it is accurate.

- Write on the whole-class board two or three ways of spelling a word, one of which is correct, e.g.

  wos   woz   was   whas

- Ask the children to write on their mini-whiteboards the spelling which they think is accurate.
- Use words that the class often misspell, e.g. because, they, February, answer, ache, tomorrow, beginning, creature, mystery, chocolate, etc.

- Discuss the different methods that can be used to remember spellings. See what memory-joggers the children already use. How are they going to remember the words you've just discussed?
- Try to ensure that the most common 'tricky' words are really well known. Examples include:

> about, after, again, all, another, away, because, brother, called, can't, could/would/should, don't, first, friend, girl, half, here, house, how, laugh, little, made, many, more, next, night, now, off, once, our, people, said, saw, school, sister, their, there, they're, these, they, three, to, too, two, very, water, were, what, when, where, who, will, with, your

Encourage the children to use the tactics explored here when proof-reading their own writing. It can help if they get used to putting a dotted line under any word that they think looks 'incorrect' as they write. This means that they can keep on writing without losing pace, and get used to returning to words after composition is complete.

PHOTOGRAPH

This game is simple to organise. It is a whole-class version of the famous 'look/say/remember/cover/think/write/check' routine. It helps to strengthen children's visual memory of different spellings.

- Write on the whole-class board a word that is commonly causing problems for the group, e.g.

because

- Ask the children to look at the word and chant the letters, trying to remember what the word LOOKS like and how it is spelled. I often suggest that they 'take a photo' (i.e. make a visual or mental note). It is worth asking them to look and then close their eyes – can they SEE the word in their mind?
- Practise this a few times before eventually covering the word completely. Ask the class to write the word on their mini-whiteboards and then to check what they've written carefully. Does it look right? Does it read back correctly? If not, change it!
- You might like to try this game with some of the trickier keywords that children need to be able to spell. Examples include:

> above, across, almost, along, also, always, animals, any, around, asked, baby, balloon, before, below, better, between, birthday, both, brother, bought, brought, can't, change, children, clothes, coming, didn't, different, does, don't, during, earth, every, eyes, father, first, follow, found, friends, garden, goes, great, halves, happy, head, heard, high, I'm, important, inside, jumped, knew, know, lady, leave, light, money, they, said, was, Tuesday, Wednesday, Thursday, Friday, Saturday, February, August, December

Try to encourage the children to use a variety of spelling strategies, e.g. visual memory-joggers, thinking about other words that may be related or similar, and so on.

RHYME IT

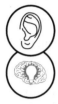

This game is important because it tunes children into listening carefully to the sounds in a word. Being able to spell by analogy (if I can spell 'sick' then I can probably spell 'stick') is a tactic that most of us use – probably without knowing it.

- Write a word on the whole-class board and ask the class to come up with as many rhyming words as they can in a given time, e.g. 30 seconds. For instance, you might write up

  feet

  and the children will then generate rhyming words, thinking about their spelling as they write them down. Of course, here there is a choice between 'ee', 'ea' or 'e consonant e' (sleet, meat, seat, treat, wheat, heat, complete, etc).
- Bring the class together and list the words they've come up with. (Sadly, on this occasion, there are no rules that help distinguish whether a word is spelt 'eat', 'eet' or 'ete'. You just have to learn each spelling through constantly memorising, using and double-checking them.
- Try using the following words to generate rhymes:

  train, wheel, bone, light, flies, soap, seed, snail, sign, goat, cream, face, five, bowl, cake, hook, wing, car, sock, back, shout, wood, led, bad, toy, day, gate, see, try, blow, true

- An extension of this game is to provide a 'rime' and let the children generate words within a given time, e.g. ake = cake, lake, bake, make, take, mistake, etc. Try using the following 'rimes':

ake, ame, ave, ace, ate, ail, ain, ine, ipe, ice, ight, oon, ool, oast, eet

- Play 'rhyme chain' – one child says a word and the next has to find a rhyme. Keep going till the rhymes run out.
- Those who struggle with spelling may need to play 'phoneme fingers'. Like the rhyming activities above, this game helps to strengthen children's listening skills in an effort to improve spelling. In this game, you say a word, e.g. 'ship' and the children have to count silently the number of phonemes (individual sounds) and hold up the relevant number of fingers, e.g. 3 (sh-i-p has 3 sounds but the first 'sh' is represented by two letters).

SPEEDWRITE

This game helps children learn how to spell a word through kinaesthetic learning. It is a simple enough idea, but the technique has proved to be very effective.

- Write on the whole-class board a word that is of interest or causing concern. Look at the word together considering different ways in which it might be learned – maybe there is a useful rhyme, perhaps it follows a pattern, could there be a mnemonic to help you remember it?
- Once you've considered ways to recognise it, ask the children to write down the word as many times as possible within 30 seconds – with the correct spelling. This is most powerful

if they use joined-up handwriting – the hand eventually learns the pattern of a word.

- Try working on words that all share a common pattern. For instance, you might decide to focus on 'would', 'should' and 'could'. There are endless groups that share patterns. Pick up on common patterns that the children find difficult. Also, focus on patterns given in the school scheme of work – both the current objectives, as well as those from previous terms if they have not been learned. Here are a few examples to get things started:

> might, fight, right, sight, bright, flight
> foam, moan, groan, road, coast, float
> slow, know, narrow, borrow, below, follow, elbow
> jumped, leaped, wanted, cried, frightened
> sing, bring, king, wing, sling, running, fling
> slowly, calmly, quickly, angrily, happily
> curtain, fountain, captain, mountain, certain
> caught, taught, daughter, naughty

Do not underestimate how many times children have to spell a word correctly before that word becomes part of their automatic vocabulary. Of course, it helps if they really need that word in their writing, as this will give them a real purpose for spelling it correctly.

FINISH

This game is handy for children who struggle with spelling, as it provides them with a scaffold in the form of letters already being in place.

- Start by writing up parts of a word on the whole-class board and give the children a fixed amount of time – say 20 seconds – to complete the word. Sometimes they will be able to make several words. For instance,

st__p

could be 'stamp', 'stop', 'stoop', 'steep', 'strip', 'strap', etc.
- You might want to use a dash to represent each missing letter. This narrows the options down, so give the children less time to work it out. An example could include:

v_ry

in which case the answer could only be 'very' or 'vary'.
- You could choose a group of words where a choice of 'fillings' has to be made. For instance, you might write 'ur', 'ir', 'er' and 'ear' on the whole-class board.
- Now provide some words with a space and see if the class can decide which letters are required to complete the word, e.g.

th_ _st

The answer is, of course, 'ir' ('thirst'). With this group of sounds, you could also use the following words:

'ur' – surprise, urgent, purchase, furniture, purpose, survive
'ir' – circle, dirt, bird, squirt
'er' – service, member, nerve, offer, letter
'ear' – search, early

- As an extension to this, try words that use the following sounds:

'oi' or 'oy'   – boy, spoil, etc.
'or', 'au' or 'aw' – snore, caught, paw, etc.
'ou' or 'ow'   – sound, prow, etc.
'oo', 'ue' or 'ew' – smooth, blue, crew, etc.
'f', 'ff', 'ph' or 'gh' – fat, cuff, phone, cough, etc.

SPELLING RIDDLES

This is great fun to play because it involves a 'riddling' element while leading into spelling. The idea is to provide two or three clues to a word which the children have to guess.

- Decide on what sort of words the class will be focusing on, e.g. words with double consonants in them, such as 'lorry', 'swimming', etc.
- Choose one of these words and provide two or three clues, asking the children to guess what it is. If you were to choose 'rubbish', for example, you might give the following clues:

'This word has a double consonant. In America it is called "trash", and some

people might call things that are broken a
load of . . .'

- For the word 'running' you might say:

  'This word is a fast movement. It has a
  double "n" in it and you are not supposed
  to do it along the corridor.'

WORDS IN WORDS

 Another popular game is to look for words within
words.

- Think of a handful of words that incorporate
  other shorter words and write these on the
  whole-class board, e.g. 'begin' has hidden in it
  five words – be, beg, gin, I, in.
- See who can find the hidden word(s). Give a
  rapid time limit so that the children really have
  to work hard, looking carefully at the selection
  you've given them. Setting a group the task of
  collecting words with words inside them is a
  simple way of building up your own store to
  use with the class!
- Try these words and add more to the list:

  because, friend, pamphlet, whisper, goldfish . . .

- A related game is to write a long word on the
  whole-class board and provide a set time for the
  children to write words made up from the
  letters. This exercise can go on for a long time.
  Use 'antidisestablishmentarianism' as a starter!

WHICH IS WHICH?

This game focuses on words that children often muddle up, e.g. 'were' and 'where'.

- Begin by selecting the words that the children are prone to muddling. Write the words on the whole-class board and see if there are tricks for remembering which one to use, e.g.

  'Here' is easily distinguished from 'hear' because 'hear' has an 'ear' at the end!

- Having discussed strategies for remembering which is which, say a sentence containing one of these words and ask the class to write down on their mini-whiteboards which spelling they think is correct. Try focusing on:

  here, hear
  where, were, wear
  to, too, two
  there, their, they're
  of, off

WORD BLOCKS

This activity lends itself to being either an oral or written exercise, and is a fun way to encourage children to think about word formation and spelling.

- On the whole-class board, draw a simple grid containing nine letters (or more). You need at least one vowel.
- The object of the game is for the class to combine the letters, making as many words as

possible. For example, your grid might contain the letters

S	T	P
A	O	L
B	M	R

in which case 'stop', 'stab', 'stamp' and 'star' are just a few of the words that could be generated. Children can be asked to write them down individually or in small groups, or to give their answers out loud (the last option guarantees a raucous and exciting session).

WHAT IS THE RULE?

You will need: A selection of reading books, dictionaries (enough for one between two).

This game helps children learn how to spell words through thinking about possible rules or conventions. While it is tempting to tell children a rule, learning is all the more powerful when they problem solve these conventions for themselves.

- Write a list of words on the whole-class board and ask the children to work in pairs to generate the rule that relates to them. As most rules have exceptions, you might extend the game by searching for these in books, dictionaries, or through brainstorming.
- Give the children the following list of words. See if they work out the rule for changing the words on the left to those on the right (the rules have been supplied for you alongside).

move – moving
shove – shoving
change – changing
come – coming
love – loving

> *Remove the 'e' and add 'ing'*

- What is the rule for these words?

hop – hopping
slip – slipping
tap – tapping
step – stepping
shut – shutting

> *Double the final consonant after a short vowel sound and add 'ing'*

- As an extension to this activity, see if the children can guess what the different prefixes or suffixes mean by looking at the words containing them. For example, give the class the words 'misadventure', 'misbehave', 'misfortune', 'mislay', 'mislead', 'misprint', 'mistake' and ask them to decide what the prefix 'mis' means (answer = wrong). Repeat the exercise using the following prefixes/ suffixes (the answers have been provided for you):

Prefixes
'ante-' (before)
'anti-' (against)
'dis-' (not or away)
'ex-' (out of)
'inter-' (between)
'pre-' (before)
'sub-' (under)
'trans-' (across)

Suffixes
'-able' or '-ible' (capable of being)
'-ess' (female)
'-hood' (state of being)
'-less' (without)
'-ous' (full of)

HOMONYMS AND HOMOPHONES

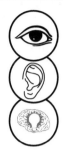

You will need: photocopies of the poem 'Sought it out!' (p. 14) (one for each child).

This activity is divided into two parts. The first game looks at words that share the same spelling but have different meanings. These are known as 'homonyms'.

- The aim here is to create funny sentences using the different meanings, e.g.

  The **bat** grabbed the **bat** and batted the ball.

- Try using these homonyms to create sentences: watch, sink, trip, arm, match, jam, fan, rock, back, light.
- Encourage the children to draw pictures to help them remember these homonyms. For instance, a picture of a footballer wearing odd socks could be used to illustrate the following sentence:

  His socks didn't **match** at the football **match**.

The next game looks at words that sound the same but have different spellings, e.g. 'made' and 'maid'. These are known as 'homophones'.

- Brainstorm a list of homophones with the children, writing their suggestions on the whole-class board.
- Just as you did with the homonyms, invite the class to try using the new words in funny sentences of their own, e.g.

  The **hare** had spiky **hair**.

- Give each child a copy of the poem 'Sought it out!'. Look at the poem together, reading it through and deciding which homophones are being used (don't forget the one in the title!).
- Write similar sentences to the ones in the poems, following the same pattern.

SOUGHT IT OUT!

The rider pulled on the rain
(and got soaking wet for his trouble).

He rowed to the key
(it opened but he could not land).

He tried to sew a pattern
(but nothing grew in the field).

He combed his hare
(but it struggled to escape).

He followed its cent
(and had enough to pay for a pair).

He cooked fresh bread with flower
(and ate a primrose loaf).

He sheltered beneath an old yew
(but its bleating woke him).

He watched the night put on his spurs
(they gleamed like stars).

He climbed the Queen's stare to bed
(and slept in her eyes).

He was pleased to reach the end of the tail
(to his surprise it wagged happily).

Pie Corbett

REVERSIBLES

You will need: dictionaries and/or reading books.

- Hold a two-minute search for reversible words, e.g.

pat	$\rightarrow$	tap
snip	$\rightarrow$	pins
strap	$\rightarrow$	parts
ward	$\rightarrow$	draw

Suggest to the children that they should list as many 3 and 4 letter words as they can. Then to check for any that are reversible!
- An extension of this activity would be to explain to the children that there are certain words that read the same backwards as they do forwards, e.g. 'eye', 'level', 'radar', 'noon'. These sorts of words are called 'palindromes'. If anyone in the group is called 'Anna' or 'Hannah' or 'Bob', their names are palindromes too!

WORD LADDERS

This is an excellent word-building activity and can be a useful way of developing vocabulary and improving spelling.

- First decide whether the word ladders will be general or themed – you could either use any old words or go for a category (which is harder).
- The aim of the game is to make a list of words within a given time. Participants do this by

making sure that the last letter of each word becomes the first of the next word. For instance:

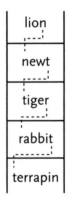

An animal ladder would run as follows:

SHANNON'S GAME

This is a variation of the well-known game of 'Hangman'. The only difference between 'Shannon's game' and 'Hangman' is that in 'Shannon's game' the letters have to be guessed in the right order. This develops a sense of 'serial probability' – a key spelling skill which involves thinking about what is the most likely letter or letter combination to come next. For instance, if a word begins with the letters 'st', the third letter is unlikely to be a 'b' and more likely to be a vowel.

- Play this game in exactly the same way as 'Hangman'. You will need to draw a set number of dashes to indicate the number of letters in your chosen word.
- Children take it in turns to suggest the next letter. You can challenge them by asking what word they are thinking of. If they do not guess correctly, then another part of the hangman's gallows is drawn (if you find the idea of a hangman's gallows too ghoulish then draw something else, e.g. a face). You will find that getting the first few letters is the hardest. As the word emerges, letter by letter, the number of choices narrows. If the class struggle to get going, provide them with the first letter.

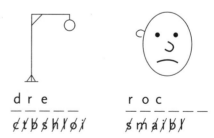

CHAPTER 2
Jumpstarting words

Word games are handy for generating an excitement about words and how they work. The games in this chapter playfully focus on different word classes in a lively manner that is light years away from the dull grammar exercises that used to torture me when I was at school! I have found that generating an interest in words and how they work can develop a love of language in children. They are fun, but you also need to think hard!

RIDDLING WITH NOUNS

Riddling, as we saw in the previous chapter, can be superb fun and is a real favourite with children. This activity focuses on 'concrete nouns' (i.e. people, places, or things).

- Choose a category, e.g. food, names, animals. Write the letters of the alphabet on the whole-class board. The class now have two minutes to come up with as many words as they can within that category – one noun for each letter of the alphabet. For example, supposing the category were food, the children might come up with something like this:

  a – apricot b – banana c – cake d – damson . . .

- To make the activity more visual use a picture or object as the starting point, e.g. bring in a banana for 'food'!

- An alternative is to write a word such as 'dog' or 'cat' on the whole-class board and give the children 30 seconds to list as many alternatives, e.g. Poodle, Alsatian, Rottweiler and so on.
- Play an oral riddle game in which the answer is a noun. Start by asking someone to think of a noun (which they should keep to themselves initially), e.g. 'bus'. The volunteer then reveals, one by one, clues, e.g.

> These travel on roads
> They can have two decks
> The ones in London are red . . .

The first person to guess the noun swaps over and the game starts again!

ACTING VERBS

You will need: thesauruses (enough for one between two).

This little game helps to tune children into thinking about varying the verbs they use. Good writing often hinges on choosing a powerful verb.

- Brainstorm alternative words for 'look', 'said', 'went', 'got', 'ate', 'touch'. Who can come up with the most in 30 seconds?

look	– peer, stare, glare, gaze, glance, peek, etc.
said	– muttered, whispered, yelled, shrieked, snarled, etc.
went	– rushed, dashed, crept, bounded, etc.
got	– climbed, clambered, grabbed, etc.
ate	– munched, chewed, tasted, nibbled, etc.
touch	– poke, prod, stroke, punch, tickle, etc.

- You can vary this game by using a thesaurus. In pairs, the children have 30 seconds to find and list alternatives on their mini-whiteboards.
- Next ask the children, individually or in pairs/small groups, to act out one of the verbs while the rest of the class write down on their mini-whiteboards what they think the verb might be.

TALKING ADVERBS

This is a perfect extension of the previous game. An exercise of this sort really gives children the impetus and confidence to make their own writing more colourful and interesting.

- Take a simple sentence that someone might speak, e.g. 'Do you think it might snow?' or 'Has anyone seen my glasses?' and write it on the whole-class board, followed by the words 'he said', 'she said', 'Harvinder said', etc.
- Brainstorm a list of adverbs that might go with the word 'said', e.g. 'uneasily', 'calmly', 'slowly', 'softly', 'quietly', 'loudly', etc.
- Children take it in turns to say the sentence in the manner of one of the adverbs and others have to guess which one is being used. Use the same game for speech verbs, e.g. 'snarled', 'snapped', 'hissed', 'whispered', 'bellowed', etc.

IN THE MANNER OF THE WORD

This is an alternative adverb game in which children attempt to physically represent chosen adverbs which a volunteer then tries to guess.

- Start by outlining the various steps of the activity to give the children an idea of what is involved.
- Next ask for a volunteer to be the 'adverb guesser'.
- Once chosen, this child leaves the room while everyone else agrees on an adverb, e.g. 'slowly'.
- The child is called back into the room and asks others to act out something 'in the manner of the word' they have just chosen, e.g. they might be asked to 'walk across the room' or to 'sing a nursery rhyme'. This would then have to be done in the manner of the adverb, i.e. slowly.
- The child then tries to guess the adverb based on the actions just seen.

FACE THE ADJECTIVE

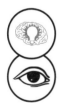

You will need: an object (e.g. a watch, an old shoe, etc.) or an enlarged picture (e.g. of a castle, a ship at sea, a candle, etc.).

Ok, this might seem slightly out of the ordinary, but the key to this tried-and-tested activity is enthusiasm! As in all things, enthusiasm from the teacher equals enthusiasm from the children, so GO FOR IT!

- Making sure that everyone in the room can see you, make a face and ask the children to jot down on their mini-whiteboards an adjective to describe your expression, e.g. sad, lonely, aggressive, etc. Share answers once everyone has finished.

- Next call for volunteers – there should be plenty of willing participants! Let the children have fun making expressive faces.
- An alternative is to use an object or picture and to see if the children can come up with adjectives to describe it. From their suggestions create a 'word shower' on the whole-class board. If you're using a picture, pin it to the board and scatter adjectives around the outside, e.g.

hot

flickering   *yellow*

brilliant   *golden*

busy   *shimmering*

cold   *motionless*

white   *slender*

upright   *greasy*

still

PREPOSITIONS

You will need: an object or picture (see previous game for suggestions).

This game is simple to organise and can produce some really imaginative pieces of writing. It encourages children to think about setting the scene in their writing using prepositions.

- Choose a starting point based on the object or picture on display and write a sentence on the whole-class board, e.g.

  Out on the ocean, there sailed a ship.

- On their mini-whiteboards, the children have to write a description in which every line starts with a preposition, e.g.

  On the ship's deck, is a barrel of water.
  Beside the ship, drift endless waves.
  Above the deck, huge sails billow in the
    wind.

- Discuss the prepositions that have been used in the exercise and list these on the board. The activity can be repeated as many times as you like using different objects/pictures as starting points.

CONNECTIVES

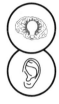

Children love this quick oral game because they really have to think. Sometimes the results can be spectacularly funny!

- Create an endless oral story in which the children take turns to say a line which they then hand on by suggesting a connective, e.g.

Child 1:	**Once** there was a miller **who**
Child 2:	spent many days cutting corn **because**
Child 3:	he needed it to bake his loaves **while**
Child 4:	his daughter prepared the yeast **after** . . .

- The first time you try this, it's a good idea to put up the first sentence yourself. Once the children have got the hang of the game, they can start the stories off themselves.

COLLECTIVE NOUNS

This activity is an amusing way to familiarise children with collective nouns, and can be used to show them how groups or collections of people or things can be described in lots of unusual and imaginative ways.

- Invent alphabets of collective nouns, grouping suggestions for each letter on the whole-class board. Various websites can be found by going through most search engines (Google has always proved to be particularly fruitful) and typing in 'collective nouns'. It seems that there are a large number of obsessive collective noun collectors out there (an anorak of collective noun collectors!). Here are a few invented examples to start you off:

An **a**bandonment of orphans
An **a**bsence of waiters
An **a**ccompaniment of condiments
An **a**ddition of mathematicians
An **a**genda of tasks
An **a**mble of walkers
An **a**nnoyance of mobile phones

- Making up collective nouns is fun. Try inventing ones that include opposites, e.g.

A hammer blow of feathers
A kiss of guns
A toast of poison
A stillness of runs

FAST POEM

This quick game follows on from the previous games and helps children think about using adjectives, adverbs and verbs effectively to create a mini poem. It could be a whole-class, group, paired, or individual activity. Poems can be written on mini-whiteboards, or you could scribe suggestions on the whole-class board.

Choose a subject (e.g. spaghetti) and then use the following framework for creating a 'fast poem': 1 noun/2 adjectives/3 adverbs/4 verbs, e.g.

Spaghetti	(1 noun)
Thin and soft,	(2 adjectives)
Silently, slowly, easily,	(3 adverbs)
Slipping, sliding, slithering, disappearing.	(4 verbs)

COMPOUND WORDS

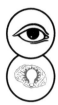

Compound words are words that are made up of two or more other words. For this game we are particularly interested in the 'closed form' of compound words, e.g. 'bedroom', 'downstairs', 'football', etc.

- Provide a list of compound words on the whole-class board. The idea is that the children make a new compound word and provide a definition for it, e.g. 'jellyground' is a term used to describe a boggy area where the ground is soft and wobbles when walked upon. Here are some words to get you going:

play	ground
air	port
jelly	fish
under	ground
over	use
news	paper
whole	meal
class	room
out	side
window	pane

- Make your list of compound words as long as possible. Then ask the children to write stories, individually or in pairs, using as many of the compounds as they can, but swapping the parts of the compound around, e.g.

classroom	roomclass
playground	groundplay

- Now read the stories aloud (an example is given below with the compound words highlighted in bold).

Last **endweek** Sam visited her **parentsgrand**.

On **daysun** morning she was eating **fastbreak** with her **mothergrand**. They were tucking into a **fruitgrape** when they heard a noise.

It was **bodysome** or **thingsome** tapping by the **bindust**. Sam rushed **longhead** and fell over. She hurt **selfher** and was looking at a torn **nailfinger** when she saw what had been making the noise.

It was a **somehand** frog trying to eat a **wormearth**. As soon as it saw Sam it leaped onto the **boardcup** and across the **boardside**. It even tried to jump **stairsup**. Sam chased it.

Mothergrand screamed. 'This is not a **groundplay**! Stop playing with that frog before your **fathergrand** comes **stairsdown** and sees it.'

At that moment the frog played **frogleap** out of the window.

Sam leaped like a **keepergoal** but it was too late. Her **somehand** prince was gone!

HIDE AND SEEK WORDS

I've known some children become besotted with this game. It builds on the earlier 'Words in words' game (p. 9), but is more difficult.

Write the passage below on a whole-class board, OHP or photocopiable sheet that can be copied and given to each child. The sentences in the passage contain words that have their beginning in one word and their end in the next. Can the children find the hidden words? The first is done for them, i.e. 'Some where' has 'mew' hidden in it.

So**me w**here in these sentences there are hidden words that have their beginning in one word and their end in the next word. Look carefully and you will notice that there are quite a mixture of words to pick from, so pay close attention to the appearance of the alphabet.

ALPHABETS

We used to play this game endlessly when I was at primary school and, some years later, it's still a hit with children.

- Write the alphabet down the side of the whole-class board, or photocopiable sheet (if you intend the children to work individually).
- Along the top write headings for different categories, e.g. boys' names, girls' names, etc. Ask the class to complete the alphabet for each category (as far as possible) within a given time, e.g.

Boys' names		*Girls' names*
A	Ahmed	Aisha
B	Benjamin	Becky
C	Connor	Chang
D	Daniel	Daisy

CAR NUMBER PLATES

The aim of this game is to make up short sentences using words that begin with the letters from car number plates.

- Before playing the game, collect various number plates (the teachers' car park is a good place to start). To make the whole exercise even more interesting, ask the children to collect a few number plates on their way to and from school.
- Write the letters on the whole-class board, e.g. my car is B D D. Try to include as many sets of letters as possible.
- Now see if the children can invent a short sentence using words that start with the letters on the board, e.g.

  Bill **D**ug **D**eep.

- Sentences can be written on mini-whiteboards and shared at the end of the activity.

ANAGRAMS

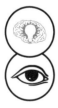

You will need: an enlarged copy of the anagrams poem (see below), or individual copies for each child.

This activity can create an interesting buzz to get a session underway.

- Stick the enlarged copy of the anagrams poem on the whole-class board, or give the individual copies out to the children.
- Who can work out what is happening in each mini verse? Can anyone suggest an appropriate title? Examples could include 'All shook up' or 'Gramanas' (an anagram of anagram!).

The eyes –
They see.

Astronomers
See
No more stars.

Astronomers
Are
Moon-starers.

Angered is
Enraged.

My mother-in-law
Is
The warm lion.

The orchestra
Is a
Carthorse.

Let the organ
Groan.

A suitable punishment
Is
Nine thumps.

Sauciness
Causes sin.

- Anagrams are easy to generate – simply select a few words and muddle the letters. Then it is a matter of heads down and see who can sort the letters into words. Show the children how you would tackle it. For instance it can help to put the letters in a circle as follows:

```
              A

      M             N

   A                   A

      R    G
```

- It can help if all the words in a series of
  anagrams fall into the same category, e.g.
  animals. Just to get you going, try these creature
  anagrams (answers have been given):

peanlote	(antelope)
the lean p	(elephant)
grite	(tiger)
inlo	(lion)
aberz	(zebra)
adnap	(panda)
we steel dib	(wildebeest)
oitrotse	(tortoise)

- Now look carefully at these anagrammatic
  riddles. The first line is the anagram and the
  second line is a clue. Answers can be found
  below!

  (1) A vocal ruby
       Is your wordstore.

  (2) Toes in evil
       Will give you square eyes.

  (3) The plane
       Is a vast creature.

  (4) Ken glowed
       As he knew so much.

(5) Foes rant on
Always after twelve.

(6) O pity slim ibis
For this cannot be done.

Answers: (1) vocabulary, (2) television,
(3) elephant, (4) knowledge, (5) afternoons,
(6) impossibility

CHAPTER 3
Jumpstarting sentences

This chapter includes lots of games that make good starters for lessons. In the main, they are concerned with helping children develop the skills needed to construct and vary sentences with speed and accuracy. This is a key writing skill, and it is worth remembering that children who have not yet mastered the art of sentence writing will struggle with composing whole texts. Many of the games encourage children to be inventive while developing their own written style.

MUCKING ABOUT WITH A SENTENCE

This game helps children gain control over varying and constructing sentences.

When I was asked to write some activities for the National Literacy Strategy in 2000 I had several that came under the general heading of 'mucking about with sentences'. The NLS folk didn't mind, but you can imagine what the Ofsted terriers thought of it ('mucking about' was NOT permitted – they wanted serious analysis . . .). It was sometimes like standing at the gates of Hades and feeling the sad, hot breath of Death itself, reaching out to stultify and terrorise any sign of creativity, imagination or initiative that teachers and children might have. Still, here is the fun game called 'mucking about with sentences' – at long last!

- Ask the class to write a sentence on their mini-whiteboards. To get things going, you could all play the game together using a sentence written on the whole-class board, e.g.

  The cat ran along the wall.

- Now take out the verb ('ran') – how does it sound?
- Now put the verb back in and add some adjectives or an adverb, e.g.

  The *sleek* cat ran *carelessly* along the *mossy* wall.

- Now take out the nouns, e.g.

  The sleek ran carelessly along the mossy.

- Now extend the sentence using 'because', e.g.

  The sleek ran carelessly along the mossy because the next door neighbour's dog was barking.

- Shift the end to the beginning, e.g.

  Because the next door neighbour's dog was barking, the sleek ran carelessly along the mossy.

- Move the adverb, e.g.

  Carelessly, because the next door neighbour's dog was barking, the sleek ran along the mossy.

- Keep on playing in this manner, making up sentences, listening to the impact. Add in techniques such as:

Alliteration	The cool, crafty cat ran recklessly along the white, wobbly wall.
Simile	The cat, as quick as a tick, ran along the wall like a cheetah.
Personification	The wall bent over and itched its back.

- Try altering the sentence type, turning it into the following:

A question	Why did the cat run along the wall?
An exclamation	Cat – scat!
A compound sentence	The cat ran along the wall and the rat ran along the path.
A complex sentence	The cat ran along the wall as it had spied a flying fish.

- Try turning the basic sentence into different text types, e.g.

Recipe	Leave the cat to run along the wall for a minute.

Newspaper	Last night a wild cheetah was sighted on the town wall.
Discussion	Locally, there is much debate about whether or not we should allow cats to run on the town walls.
Report	At night, cats like to roam. They will even walk along the walls.

MAKING SENTENCES

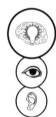

In this game children work on their ability to construct sentences confidently and automatically. It doesn't require much preparation (just make sure the children have their mini-whiteboards at the ready), and it can be played in several different ways depending on which skills you want to exercise (visual, auditory, etc.).

- Write a word on the whole-class board, e.g. **'snake'**. The children have to write a sentence containing this word rapidly on their mini-whiteboards. Be ruthless – their sentence must have a full stop, capital letter and it must make sense. Also, insist that they reread them before holding up their board for you to see. Give them the following sentence as an example:

    The **snake** slithered along the top of the sand dune.

- To make this game more visual, use pictures or objects instead of words. To make it an aural starter, use a tape recorder to play a clip of sound, e.g. a creaking door.

- A next step on is to write two words on the whole-class board. I don't move on to this stage until I'm sure the children have mastered the previous method and are ready for a new challenge. Try using two words that do not seem to go together, e.g. 'jelly' and 'shark'. This will generate some funny sentences – but warn the children to watch out. As soon as the brain becomes excited about the sentence, they run the risk of forgetting the full stop!

- When checking the children's whiteboards, make sure that everyone always uses a capital letter and full stop. Get the children to 'police' their own sentences, encouraging them to be 'strict' with themselves! Sometimes I say, 'pretend you are me – you know what I am looking for'. You will also pick up on spelling errors – especially those where you know that you have already taught the pattern. If some children finish ahead of others, give them an extra challenge, e.g. add in a word, choose a 'better' word, extend the sentence using 'because', etc.

- Now start with three (or more) words that do not seem to go together, e.g. 'jelly', 'shark', 'sneezed'. You can see now that you could focus on using adverbs or adjectives or prepositions. I always prefer to practise using connectives with nouns (e.g. 'because', 'jelly', 'shark') as this helps the children compose complex sentences.

- This game is most powerful when the sorts of words used relate to the type of text that they are writing. For instance, when composing discussion writing, it is handy to practise sentences that might be useful, e.g. 'I believe that . . .', 'We have been discussing whether or not . . .', 'On the other hand . . .' and so on.

- Look out for interesting sentences or well-chosen words within the children's writing. Contrast these with dull and obvious choices, perhaps by inventing your own examples. Ask them which is better? Why? How can we change the words to make them more interesting?

CREATING SEVERAL SENTENCES

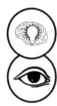

Once the class have become skilled at creating a single sentence from a given number of words it is time to move on to writing 1, 2, or 3 or more sentences from a set of words.

- Start by choosing a selection of words, all of which fit into a single category, e.g. animals. The set should include a connective , e.g. 'because', 'while', etc.
- Write the set of words on the whole-class board, e.g.

   cat
   dog
   because
   pets

- This set might lead to four sentences – a mini paragraph. If the children find using a type of word difficult (e.g. connectives) then you should model a few sentences together. When writing the sentences out, it helps if you put the connective in one colour so that it stands out. For instance, if you were practising writing 'because' sentences you might make a few up with the children, e.g.

The horse was hungry *because* it had not eaten for days.

The soldier hid *because* the enemy were approaching.

The cup was dirty *because* it had fallen in the mud.

- Of course, mini paragraphs can be made up orally in pairs, or written down. Both variations are worth playing. Once children move into putting two sentences together (i.e. one after the other) you will find that many miss out the middle full stop. Some may need to work in a pair, taking turns to write. The child who does not have the pen acts as 'fullstop policeman'!
- If this continues to be a problem, try writing sentences on the whole-class board that omit the full stop, and ask the class to punctuate them. Again, using different colours can help. Keep the exercise quick and lively.
- Think carefully about the lists of words. An unlikely combination will challenge the wit of your young writers, e.g.

  parrot
  gerbil
  violin
  while

BORING SENTENCES

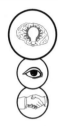

This game gets children used to thinking about the quality of the words that they use. It is about intensifying meaning – exploring the difference between the bland and the powerful, e.g.

> The man got in the car.
> (*A bit on the dull side* $^{z}z_{z}z^{z^{z}}z_{z}z^{z}$!)

or

> Pavarotti squeezed into a Skoda.
> (*That's more like it – much more interesting!*)

- Write up a dull sentence, e.g.

  The mouse ate the cheese.

- Challenge the children to improve it. Explain to them that, interestingly, there are only a few things that can be done to improve a sentence, e.g.

  1. *Add words in*: The *greedy* mouse *carefully* ate the *stale* cheese.
  2. *Add on at the end*: The mouse ate the cheese *because it was hungry.*
  3. *Add on at the beginning*: *While it was waiting,* the mouse ate the cheese.
  4. *Change words*: The *rodent gnawed* the *cheddar.*
  5. *Add in a simile*: The mouse, *like a tiny vampire,* sank its teeth into the cheese.
  6. *Alliterate*: The *mincing* mouse *marvelled* at the *mouldy* cheese *cheerfully.*

FINISHING SENTENCES

In this game you provide the class with a beginning, a middle, or an end of a sentence and they have to try to complete it. You could play this orally or using mini-whiteboards – individually, in pairs, or as a whole class.

- Start by providing openings to be completed. Write a selection of these on the whole-class board, giving one or two examples to get the children going, e.g.

    The old king . . .
    The children arrived at the . . .

- Then give them a few endings, e.g.

    . . . into the sack.
    . . . it was empty!

- Finally, see how they cope with middles (some might find this quite difficult and will need plenty of help), e.g.

    . . . jumped over . . .
    . . . changed into . . .

- A different version of this game involves working at using a broader range of connectives than 'and'. Provide a simple sentence opening, e.g. 'The sad queen sat down . . .' along with a list of conjunctions. Here are some of the most useful:

after	as	as soon as
because	before	but
once	since	so/so that
until	when	whenever
where	wherever	while

41

- The children write the sentence opening on their mini-whiteboards, select a conjunction from the list and complete the sentence, e.g. 'The sad queen sat down because it was hot.' Again, it can be helpful if they use different colours for the connectives.
- A variation of this game that offers a more puzzling challenge is to provide sentence fragments, e.g. 'rushed crazily', which the children have to complete, e.g. 'The diamonds rushed crazily through my hair.' The odd combinations can give rise to some incredibly surreal and inventive sentences! As long as they are grammatically sound, 'crazy' sentences are fine. To play this game I search through books and pick out odd combinations. Here are some, randomly chosen for you to try out:

    dancing spots
    rage echoed
    cloud of
    library was
    furious snowball

SENTENCE DOCTOR

This is a handy exercise for helping children learn how to proof-read their own writing. It works well as an oral or written exercise.

- Write up sentences that contain specific errors. I try to feed off the sorts of common errors that pupils make, e.g. omitting words and punctuation, putting commas in the wrong place, muddling up punctuation, forgetting capital letters, incorrect spelling, lack of subject-verb agreement, incorrect past tense (*we was*), use of local dialect (*it was well good*), etc.

- You could start by simply writing sentences one at a time on the whole-class board. Once the children get good at spotting errors and correcting them it is then time to build up the number of sentences until they can rapidly proof-read and improve an entire paragraph. You could provide sentences/paragraphs on a photocopiable sheet.
- Start with single sentences, e.g.

   The frog wos silent.

- Then try pairs of sentences that have been incorrectly run together, e.g.

   Two bees settled on the flowers it was their lucky day.

- Next, move on to paragraphs, e.g.

   Mr jenkins sat down.
   Would thay be late. He
   just didn't no. To past
   the time he red his
   paper.

SENTENCE COMBINATION

This game is central to helping children move beyond an overdose of 'and then'. Play it often! The idea is simple enough – all you need to do is ban the use of 'and then' during the activity.

- Provide a pair of sentences and ask the children to join them to make one sentence – without using 'and' or 'then', e.g.

   The cart stopped.
   The hobbit jumped down.

This might become:

> As the cart stopped, the hobbit jumped down.

- Try using the following words to join the sentences: as, as soon as, while, when, whenever, before, after, immediately, once, although, because, so. Other sentence combinations might focus on using the words 'why', 'what', 'how' and 'if'.

DROPPING IN

This game focuses on inserting words or clauses into sentences to enrich the meaning.

- Write a sentence on the whole-class board, e.g.

> The raft floated.

- The children then 'drop in' words as instructed, e.g. 'put in an adjective'. The result might be something like this:

> The wooden raft floated.

- Next tell them to drop in an adverb:

> The raft floated silently (*or* Silently, the raft floated).

or a prepositional phrase:

> The raft floated down the river (*or* Down the river, the raft floated).

- It is also worth practising dropping in three basic clauses:

    1. *Conjunction clauses*, which help to link ideas, e.g.

        The raft floated **because** it was well-built.

    2. *Embedded clauses*, which help us drop in more information using 'who', 'which' or 'that':

        The raft, **which was very old**, floated.

    3. '*-ing*' and '*-ed*' clauses, which help us drop in more information about a person or creature or object:

        The raft, **swirling round and round**, floated.
        The raft, **constructed by the farmer**, floated.

SENTENCE IMITATION

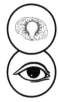

This game really helps children begin to move beyond over-relying on simple sentences. If their writing is to mature then they need to use a range of sentence types, varying them to create different effects. The following table shows different types of sentences to practise with the children. You might need to create several together before the children compose their own.

Sentence type	Reason for use	Example
Short	To build tension	*They ran.*
Long	To add information	*As the door slammed shut, Billy turned round to peer into the room, gripped his torch and advanced uneasily.*
Simple	For clarity and impact	*Camels are large animals.*
Compound	For ease and flow	*Jack was hungry and Bill was full.*
Complex	To show links between ideas and to add extra information	*After the rain stopped, they went inside.*
Question	To draw the reader in	*Do you use questions to involve the reader?*
Exclamation	To grab the reader's attention	*Make the reader sit up!*
Sentence of three for description	To set the scene	*Harry was dressed in a dark cloak, winkle-picker shoes and a flowery hat.*
Sentence of three for action	To describe what happened or to give the writing pace	*He ran down the lane, jumped over the hedge and fell flat on his nose!*
Sentence containing an 'ing' clause	To add supporting action to speech verbs	*'Yes,' said Manjit,* **turning to face the Head teacher.**

VARYING OPENINGS

This is a good activity for helping children to vary the openings to sentences. It's a great way to teach them how to add variety to their writing. You will need to model a few examples together before they try their own. An example of each technique has been provided for you.

1. Use a connective:

   While Tom waited, the bus arrived.

2. Use an 'ing' clause:

   Waiting for the others, Megan stared up at the sky.

3. Use an 'ed' clause:

   Surprised by the bang, Nadim halted.

4. Use a simile:

   Like a fish, she dived in.

5. Use an adverb:

   Carefully, she removed the bandage.

6. Use one word:

   Sad, he turned for home.

7. Use 'but' (for emphasis):

   But they were doomed.

8. Use a prepositional phrase:

   At the end of the lane, stood an old house.

POETIC SENTENCES

This is an excellent game for helping children play with language and ideas.

• Use a repeating pattern to help emphasise the idea of writing interesting sentences, e.g.

In my magic box there is a leaping lizard.
In my magic box there is a cool cloud.
In my magic box there is a terrifying tiger tickling a trout's tail.
In my magic box there is a red bus trundling along.
In my magic box there is a fingernail just like a thin moon . . .

• Other ideas for repeating lines are:

I like to look at . . .
I like to touch . . .
I like to listen to . . .
I like to taste . . .
I wish I was . . .
I want to paint . . .
What I like about . . . is . . .
Come with me and I will show you . . .
It was so quiet that I heard . . .
It's a secret but . . .
I dreamed I found . . .
In the magic mirror I saw . . .
In the room I saw . . .
Last night I dreamed . . .
To my surprise, I heard . . .
With my magic eye I saw . . .
In the rooms of dreams I found . . .
I wish I could . . .

DOING IT WITH STYLE

In this activity children have the chance to practise using different stylistic devices, including alliteration, simile and personification. You will need to model a few examples together before they try their own.

Alliteration

This is easy enough to introduce and makes for a really fun session! Start by listing some animals (e.g. tiger, lion, monkey, etc.) on the whole-class board. Then show the children how to build up a sentence using words that start with the same sound, e.g.

The lazy lion led a lingering life.

Similes

Try inventing new similes together. Write 'as thin as' on the whole-class board and ask everyone to think of very thin things. My experience is that most children will start with the more obvious objects, e.g. 'as thin as a piece of paper', '. . . a stick', '. . . a twig'. Push them to think harder. Prompt them, e.g. 'What part of an animal is very thin – its tail, a piece of hair, an eyelash?' and so on. Write a prompt list on the board, e.g. 'as tall as', 'as large as', 'as hot as', etc.

Draw some circles on the board and write a prompt above them:

The sun is like . . .

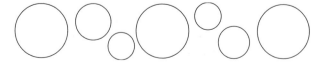

See how many other things they can think of that are round like the sun. Turn the circles on the board into the objects they suggest, e.g.

The sun is like . . .

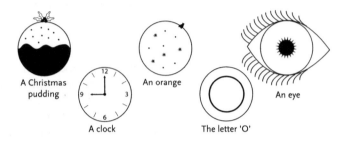

A Christmas pudding

A clock

An orange

The letter 'O'

An eye

Show them how each idea might be extended, e.g.

The sun is like
a yellow spinning wheel.

Experiment by exaggerating similes, e.g.

As slow as a snail.
As slow as a snail with its brakes on.
As slow as a snail with its brakes on stuck
in superglue!

Personification
Children love this idea. They are familiar with the classic Disney moment when magic dust is sprinkled over furniture and the objects start to dance. In essence, this is what 'personification' is – a way of bringing the world alive. The best place to do this activity is in the hall or outside. Use a flipchart or mini-whiteboards to record observations.

Make a list of objects that you can see, e.g. clock, windows, carpet, table, tree, car, etc. Then make a list of verbs – actions that humans make, e.g. laugh, giggle, grin, sneeze, walk, shuffle, dream, sleep, doze, yawn, scratch, etc.

Now marry the two lists together as if you were bringing the objects alive, e.g.

> The clock glared down and blinked its eye.
> The sofa gulped and the sink sighed.
> The windows kept silent.
> The red carpet complained because it had been trodden on.
> The table winked at the chairs.
> The desks sneezed.

SYNTACTICAL GYMNASTICS

You will need: an object or a poster.

These mini games are handy for getting the children used to controlling, altering and varying sentences.

Listing statements
Take an object (e.g. a plate of spaghetti) and give the children two minutes to write down five statements about it, e.g.

> Spaghetti is soft and thin.
> Spaghetti is a bunch of worms.

Asking questions
Write down five crazy questions you might ask the object, e.g.

> Spaghetti, where are your shoes?
> Spaghetti, why do you keep so still?

Making exclamations

Write a list of exclamations to grab the object's attention, e.g.

> Help me Spaghetti!
> Spaghetti you are a liar!

Commands

Boss the object about, e.g.

> Spaghetti, get off my plate at once.
> Spaghetti, get washed we are late.

Messages

Write or say a message for the object, e.g.

> Spaghetti, your mum wants you to go to bed early.
> Spaghetti, your teacher thinks that you should learn your alphabet.

ODD WORD = STORY

This is a story-starter game that shows children how stories can spring up from the most extraordinary places!

- Spend a few minutes brainstorming a list of nouns with the children. Write these on the whole-class board, creating a 'word wall' of suggestions. Encourage them to make their list as varied as possible . . . it will make for more imaginative stories in the long run! The word wall might look something like this:

horse	chocolate
tree	space
slipper	bath
train	scooter
kangaroo	toothpaste
clown	pumpkin

- The children each select two nouns that do not seem to go together, e.g. *horse and pumpkin* or *toothpaste and space*, and then have a few minutes to begin a narrative linking the two together. Explain to them that this was precisely what C. S. Lewis did in his classic tale, *The Lion, The Witch and The Wardrobe*. A narrative might look something like this:

  > One morning, while an astronaut was busy brushing his teeth, he noticed how beautifully white they were looking. He was due to launch off into **space** that day, so he decided to take a rocket full of **toothpaste** with him, so that he could make the stars sparkle even brighter!

WHAT IF . . .?

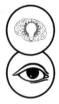

This game exercises the children's ability to pursue an idea imaginatively and sees them beginning to weave a story together. Many stories are based on a 'What if . . .?', e.g. 'What if a girl travelled to a different country through the back of a wardrobe?'

- Allow a few minutes of 'quick writing' using the following 'What if . . .?' questions as a prompt:

    What would happen if pencils could talk?
    What would happen if trees could walk?
    What would happen if dogs could fly?

- A story based on the final 'What if . . .?' might begin like this:

    <u>If dogs could fly</u>
    I was walking down to the bus stop when I heard the most extraordinary noise. It was a loud barking. Even though this is actually quite common around our neighbourhood, this barking was different. It was coming from the sky. I paused and looked up. There to my amazement was a poodle with wings flapping straight over the Post Office! Then it dived down towards the butcher's shop . . .

- As an extension get children to write 'Supposing . . .' phrases. These can act as good starting points for stories.

THE QUESTIONATOR

You will need: a poster, picture or video clip of a setting, e.g. seaside, supermarket, hospital, party, swimming pool, etc.

This is a quick-fire observation game in which children are asked to describe what's going on in a particular setting, e.g. at a supermarket, in a park, at a party, etc.

- Ask a series of questions about the setting on display. Answers could be given orally, or written speedily on mini-whiteboards, e.g.

  Who is there?
  Where are they?
  What are they doing?
  What else is there?
  What has just happened?
  What do you think might happen next?

INVENTING NEW PROVERBS

Proverbs are lots of fun to play around with. As the title of this game suggests, in this activity children have the chance to rewrite well-known proverbs to create new (and often very funny) ones of their own.

- Make a list of well-known proverbs on the whole-class board, e.g.

  An apple a day keeps the doctor at bay.
  Better to be safe than sorry.
  If at first you don't succeed, try, try again.
  Two is company, three's a crowd.
  Strike while the iron is hot.

No news is good news.
You can't teach an old dog new tricks.
The pen is mightier than the sword.

- Choose one proverb and help the children
  imitate it, changing some of the words to create
  a version of their own, e.g.

  An apple a day keeps the doctor at bay.
  A run a day keeps the flab at bay.
  A garlic a day keeps everyone at bay!

UNIVOCALICS

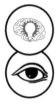

A 'univocalic' is a piece of writing that only uses
one vowel. They are not easy to write and the
children are likely to need plenty of help to
compose them. Try writing a sentence, e.g. *The three
hens went by the fence.*

- Start off by explaining what a univocalic is.
  Give the children two or three examples, e.g.

  Tom's long room took lots of work to sort.
  Jim hid his winnings in his tin.

- Help the children write their own univocalics
  on their mini-whiteboards (it may be easier if
  they do this in pairs). Share the sentences as a
  group at the end of the exericise.

MR COPYCAT

This game works well for those who struggle with language. Mr Copycat is a puppet. He says a sentence and the children have to repeat it.

- Vary the sentence type: short – long – simple – compound – complex – question – exclamation.
- Vary how the sentence is said: slow – quick – loud – soft – whisper – rhythmically – with pauses – like a robot.
- The next step is to give the children two or three sentences at a time. When the class get good at listening and imitating/repeating these, move on to sentences that the children can make their own by using the same opening (e.g. *Yesterday I saw* . . .) and adding their own ending (e.g. *Yesterday I saw a slug the size of my shoe!*).
- Another fun alternative is to choose a sentence and tell the children to pass it on, adding a word to it each time. Words can be added anywhere in the sentence. See what comes out at the end, e.g.

Teacher:	The whale swam in the sea.
Child 1:	The **monstrous** whale swam in the sea.
Child 2:	The monstrous **blue** whale swam in the sea.
Child 3:	The monstrous blue whale swam in the **deep** sea.

CHINESE WHISPERS

This is an old game which has never lost its appeal. It is ideal for times when children are in a circle, or standing in a line or queue.

Whisper a sentence, message or poem into the ear of one child. This is passed on until the last child has the message – what was it? Compare the final version with the original.

WORD BY WORD

This is a whole-class activity that children love.

- Sit the children in a circle and explain that they are going to make up sentences together, word by word, each child taking the next word.
- You put in the first word, then each child in turn has to add one word until the sentence is complete, e.g.

Teacher:	One
Child 1:	day
Child 2:	there
Child 3:	were
Child 4:	weird
Child 5:	sounds
Child 6:	coming
Child 7:	from
Child 8:	the
Child 9:	dark
Child 10:	forest.

- Try the same for story-making, inventing a sentence at a time.
- To make this more difficult, introduce a catch such as no words with the letter 'e'!

CHAPTER 4
Jumpstarting writing

This chapter pulls together a varied collection of games that make a good way to start a creative writing session. They tune the writer in to thinking imaginatively. Many of the games loosen up the mind, shaking off worries and concerns so that the children are free to think creatively. There is often no right or wrong answer – indeed, the stranger the ideas, the more the mind is beginning to roam and explore new possibilities. I find it helpful to value contributions and accept what might appear, at first, to be rather off the wall. The aim of the game is to encourage creativity, not to crush it!

INK WASTER

You will need: exercise books or mini whiteboards.

This is a great game to use at the start of a writing lesson. In many ways it is essential! It is good for loosening up inhibitions as well as creating a flow in the children's thinking and composition. It is a liberator of creative intelligence. Sometimes what they write in a minute is better than what emerges from 20 minutes of laboured writing!

The basis of the game is word association. There are two variations.

Version 1
- You suggest a title. The children have one minute to list as many words as possible on the given subject. The words don't have to be

associated or have relevance to one another, though it's a good idea to gradually move the children on to choosing words that relate more closely. After one minute, ask the class to see who has written the largest number of words.

- Begin with topics such as 'snow', 'flames', 'sea', 'darkness', 'the moon', 'night', 'traffic jams', 'lightning', etc. For 'snow', a child might write down the following:

  Snow cold white crystal blows drifts sweeps smothers flakes swarm . . .

- After a while, try to build a scene by making some suggestions, e.g. 'It is a dark night, the wind is blowing, the clouds are rushing by, the rain is lashing, thunder rumbles, lightning strikes', then tell the children the word (which in this case is 'storm'). See if they can come up with phrases based on what they have just heard. These can later be edited into poems or short descriptions.

Version 2

The second approach is to ask the children to write as much as they can about the subject in prose or poetic form. Again, this is just a matter of dashing the words down and not worrying.

The poet Katherine Gallagher uses 'ink waster'. In a recent email to me, she wrote the following:

An idea is to give students a word or a line and let them write anything with the sole proviso that they keep writing and don't lift their pen from the page. If blocked, they should repeat the mantra, 'I'm not stuck' and they'll move on. It's so important for students early on (even seven-year-olds) to get the idea and habit of flow writing.

AUTOMATIC WRITING

This is a version of 'ink waster'. I found this game in a collection of Surrealist games, on sale at Tate Britain.

- The idea is to start writing and continue without thinking, writing as fast as you can. If you stop, immediately start again by using the final letter of the last word that you wrote as the first letter of the next word. Then continue.
- It doesn't matter if the writing doesn't always tie together or you find that different sections do not relate. The idea is to let the language flow.
- Set a time limit of, say, two minutes for this activity. Begin by writing a whole-class version with children calling out ideas for each sentence or parts of sentences, which you then scribe on the whole-class board. Keep the writing rapid – if you get stuck just look at the last letter of the previous sentence and use that to get going again.
- Another version of this game is played in pairs. The game is to see which pair can write the most within a given time limit – say two minutes. On your word, the first person writes a sentence on their mini-whiteboard. The second then writes the next sentence and so on, passing the board back and forth. They need to write complete sentences – with full stops! The sense does not matter so much, though the cleverest sentences are the ones that have some sort of flow or at least create an effect!
- This can be extended even further by forming 'speed writing' teams of up to six contestants. The team members sit in a circle and take it in turns to write a word on a mini-whiteboard before passing it on to their neighbour. The

activity takes place within a set time limit – say two or three minutes. If a writer gets stuck they either use the final letter of the previous word or reuse that word to start the next sentence. Speed is of the essence. To see who has won add up the number of words each group has written.

STRANGE WORD COMBINATIONS

This is another really good game for loosening up the mind and getting words flowing. Like 'ink waster' it is based on a form of brainstorming. Begin with a whole-class example and then let the children have a go at their own word lists.

- Take a noun, e.g. dog. Write it in the centre of the whole-class board. Write a list of adjectives to the left and verbs to the right. The adjectives and verbs do not have to be associated with the dog!

shaggy		runs
angry		meows
slim		snarls
hot	dog	snaps
fat		leaps
calm		bounds
red		cries
silent		whispers

Then have fun forming the most unlikely combinations, e.g.

The red dog whispers.
The silent dog meows.

- A variation of this game could involve listing five adjectives and five verbs at random on the whole-class board, then providing a category from which the children pick their own noun. For instance, having been given 'animals' as the category, a child might choose the noun 'hippo'. The next step is to invent some strange combinations using the adjectives and verbs listed on the board.

WORD SWAP

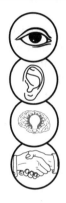

You will need: reading books.

The power of this exciting game lies in the infinite number of effects that can be created by shifting words around in sentences. The joy of it is that absolutely any sentence will do!

- Begin by selecting a sentence from any book, e.g.

   I dashed into the bathroom and brushed my teeth.

- Show the children how you can swap words over – in this instance the verbs, e.g.

   I brushed into the bathroom and dashed my teeth.

- Work on a few together as a class before letting the children have a go on their own, using sentences from their reading books. You will discover that the technique helps to trigger new and surreal effects. Try swapping verbs, adjectives, or nouns. Here is an example of noun-swapping:

In a split second he was knocked off his
feet.
In a split feet he was knocked off his
second.

- Swapping adjectives often has less of a crazy impact, but is well worth trying. A more extended activity would be to provide a passage and then ask the children to carry out a word swap. Try swapping nouns and verbs over – sometimes it helps to add in a few words and make some adjustments to verb agreement, syntax, punctuation, or meaning. For example,

  The alarm clock rang early and I jumped out of bed. I tugged on my clothes as quickly as possible. I dashed into the bathroom and brushed my teeth. Mum was calling from downstairs and a few seconds later I was downing a plate of toast.

  could become . . .

  The alarm bed rang early and I jumped out of the clock. I clothes on my tugged as possible as quickly. I brushed into the bathroom and dashed my teeth. Mum was downing from downstairs and a few seconds later I was calling a plate of toast.

  Fun, isn't it!

METAPHOR GAME

Metaphor is a powerful tool for writers. At its simplest level, a metaphor is when you say one thing *is* another, e.g. The moon is a balloon.

- In this game, choose an animal and compare it to one of the following:

  a person
  a place
  an object
  a mood
  a colour
  a number
  a vegetable
  a fruit
  a vehicle
  a TV programme
  a character from a book
  a plant
  an insect

- The metaphors can just be sheer invention. Here is a metaphor list about a giraffe.

  A giraffe is:
  a clown on stilts at the circus,
  the Eiffel Tower in Paris,
  a hat stand with no hats,
  a hopeful glance across the town,
  a yellow streak of sunset,
  the number one . . .

- You could also write metaphor lists about people, objects, animals or abstract ideas such as Anger is . . .

NONSENSE WORDS

Every child enjoys the anarchy of nonsense words – they chant them in the playground (*inky, pinky, ponky*) and love to collect silly sayings and daft words. This game capitalises on the pleasure they get from the slapstick humour of invented language.

- Write a number of words at random on the whole-class board and demonstrate how to combine bits of proper words to form new nonsense words, e.g.

   Today walked teacher bring above aggressive

   might lead to . . .

   walcher breacher abing bressive abrove

- Each child invents five new words from those on the board and then swaps these with a friend. The partner has to create nonsense sentences using the words that they have been given, e.g.

   The breacher turned to the walcher and
   twisted the abrove.
   It was bressive abing the canal boat.

- As an alternative, take a well-known poem or a passage from a book. Replace some of the keywords with invented words. For instance, the first verse of Blake's famous poem 'The Tyger' reads:

   Tyger! Tyger! Burning bright
   In the forests of the night,
   What immortal hand or eye
   Could frame thy fearful symmetry?

but you could change it to:

Breacher! Breacher! Vorpid bright
In the bressive of the night,
What abroval gurd or shork
Could grobe thy drayful stomahawk?

As this example shows, when using a poem for this activity, the effect is much more dramatic if you keep to the original format and rhythm.

PASS THE POEM

This is a good time-filler or starter and is great for getting the brain in gear. You could do a written version if you like, but it works just as well orally. Give children time to work on the ideas in pairs – 15 seconds or so should be sufficient. The key is to get the brain buzzing!

- Build up a poem with each person adding a new line. This is easiest when tackling a poem which has a repeating phrase, i.e. where all the lines begin with the same words, and children simply have to add their own ending. Invent a few together before you move on to individual or paired offerings, e.g.

  In the magic mirror I saw Tarzan resting on a lion's claw.
  In the magic mirror I saw a clause pause and sharpen its paws.
  In the magic mirror I saw a slipper rip a packet in two.
  In the magic mirror I saw a cloud yodelling.

- Other useful repeating phrases include:

  In the room I saw . . .
  Last night I dreamed . . .
  To my surprise, I heard . . .
  With my magic eye I saw . . .
  In the rooms of dreams I found . . .
  It is a secret but . . .
  I wish I could . . .

- Children should try to make each line very
  different so that the reader is surprised by the
  unexpected. They need to think hard and
  choose their words with care. At the same time,
  writing quickly helps to improve flow – so the
  trick is to concentrate meditatively and write at
  speed, keeping the brain in top gear! There's no
  need for them to worry about bits they're
  unhappy with – they can cross out anything
  they don't want to keep!

PASS THE STORY

This works in much the same way as the 'Pass the
poem' game, but the idea here is to make up a story
bit by bit.

- In this game one person begins the tale by
  writing the first sentence on a mini-whiteboard.
  They then read it to the class, group, or their
  partner.
- The children take it in turns to write the next
  sentence on their own mini-whiteboard, each
  time reading out what they've written.
- When everyone has finished, the whole story
  should be read from start to finish – with the
  children reading the sentence they have written.

- This exercise can be made more testing by adding a rule such as, 'You cannot use a word that has the letter "e" in it!'

IN THE STREET I SAW

This game is quite handy for training the memory. It also helps children to build up a scene/setting visually. The game is rather like painting a picture where you increasingly add in more detail. It is based on the old game that I used to play as a young child, 'In my Grandma's bag there is . . .'

- The idea is that one person begins by saying 'In the street I saw' and adds in an item, e.g. 'a dog'. The second player repeats what the first has said and adds in a second detail. This is passed round the class – orally – adding a new idea each time, gradually building a picture of a scene, e.g.

  > In the street I saw a dog.
  > In the street I saw a dog and a bicycle.
  > In the street I saw a dog, a bicycle, and a post box.
  > In the street I saw a dog, a bicycle, a post box, and an old man falling over . . .

- You could change scenes when the list gets too long, e.g. supermarket, seaside, city centre, back alley, kitchen, playground, train station, etc. This would be a really interesting way to explore different settings with the class. A written version of the game would also be handy for building up the idea of using commas in a list.
- Furthermore, while it's worth sticking to single nouns at the start, once the children have got

the hang of the game, show them how to make more of each noun (i.e. building a noun phrase), e.g.

> In the street I saw:
> A cat
> A ***marmalade*** cat (Add an *adjective* to describe how it looks)
> A marmalade cat ***sleeping*** (Add a *verb* to describe what it's doing)
> A marmalade cat sleeping ***in the corner*** (Add a *prepositional phrase* to describe where it is)
> A marmalade cat sleeping ***soundly*** in the corner (Add an *adverb* to describe how it's doing it)

POSTCARDS

It is worth building up a large collection of postcards. They have the advantage of providing lots of variety and can be used on many occasions as long as the children do not always use the same card. The most successful ones seem to be those of paintings. Surreal paintings work well, as do scenes where something is seen to be happening. Portraits also work well – holiday snaps of sunsets do not!

You need a varied and broad collection of postcards – somewhere in the region of 100 is ideal. The children each select a card . . . and then there are all sorts of ways that these can be used to trigger the imagination:

Book cover
1. Pretend that the card is the cover of a book. Get the children to write down the book's title on their mini-whiteboards.

2. They should then write down three possible titles and underline the best.
3. In pairs, the children take it in turns to tell their partner what the book is about.
4. Next ask them to imagine that this card is an illustration from inside a storybook. Can they explain to their partner what is happening?
5. They should then try to write the first line of the story, followed by the rest of the opening paragraph.

Wish you were here
1. Pretend that someone is about to write the postcard. Who is sending it and to whom?
2. What has just happened to the sender of the card?
3. Ask the children to imagine they are the sender. On their mini-whiteboards, see if they can write the message they are going to put on the back of the card.
4. An extension of this is to try writing the message in different ways, varying the tone depending on the sort of event they are describing, e.g. a happy event, sad, exciting, dangerous, astonishing, dull, inexplicable, etc.

Similar activities to these can be played using objects: Who does the object belong to? Why does it matter to them? Where did they get it? Who wants it and why? What is hidden inside it? The object witnessed an amazing event – what was it?

VIDEOS

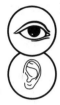

You will need: a TV and video-player, video clips and/or short programmes, enough cartoons from comics/newspapers for a paired activity.

Video is a much under-used stimulus to creativity. It is a great way to enhance children's imagination while making the learning experience fun. The possibilities are endless. Try these:

1. Play a short video clip with the sound turned down. In pairs the children have to work out the dialogue. They will need to see the clip a number of times. The dialogue should be written down on mini-whiteboards. Have fun hearing back what the children have decided the characters are saying.
2. Change the above by issuing an instruction, e.g. one of the characters is feeling – sad, angry, bossy, lonely, excited, jealous, hopeful, etc.
3. Show a short clip from the middle of a programme. The activity is for children to decide what they think has happened just before the clip – challenge them to 'tell the story' up to the clip.
4. A follow-on from this activity is for them to decide and describe what they think will happen next.
5. Play a short clip of two characters. The activity is for the children to decide how the characters feel and to explain why they think this. They should think about the characters' actions, hand movements, how they stand, their facial expressions as well as the atmosphere suggested by the weather and setting.
6. Watch a short clip with the sound on. Working in pairs, the children decide what each

character is really thinking. On whiteboards, these thoughts can be presented in cartoon form using think bubbles. The children should draw a cartoon strip of three or four boxes showing the characters from the clip with their thoughts in bubbles, each box focusing on a different stage in the video clip.

7. Dialogue can also be focused on by using cartoons with the speech bubbles blanked out. Take the cartoons that you collected before the start of the session. Blank out one or two of the bubbles in each cartoon. Working in pairs on one cartoon at a time, the children have to interpret the pictures and then decide on what the characters are saying. Depending on the cartoon chosen this can be simple or tricky. They should write their ideas down on their mini-whiteboards before swapping cartoons with another pair. The characters thoughts could be written down as follows:

BOASTING

You will need: an enlarged copy of 'Pie Corbett is . . .' (see next page), photocopies for each child (optional).

This gives children a wonderful chance to boast! Ideas can be written down, but the activity works just as well orally. The idea is to write a list of invented boasts about yourself.

- I find this works best if you make a list of basic categories as a class and write these on the whole-class board. This acts as a useful support and triggers off ideas. You could boast about:

  Sports
  Literature
  Cars
  Artists
  Films
  TV
  Cooks
  Olympics
  Places
  Inventors/inventions
  Breaking records
  Amazing creatures

- An example has been given on the next page. Stick the enlarged version of 'Pie Corbett is . . .' on the whole-class board and read it through together. You might like to photocopy it so that each child has a copy to refer back to. It's full of invented boasts about myself. Get the children to start by writing their name followed by 'is' at the top of their mini-whiteboard. Then see how many boasts they can come up with!

> ## PIE CORBETT IS . . .
>
> a Mercedes at top speed,
> an undiscovered planet,
> the first person to eat
> three Shredded Wheat
> and have space for more,
> cleverer than Einstein,
> a number one hit record,
> a regular feature in
> The Guinness Book of Records,
> a stand-in for Harry Potter,
> a cutglass chandelier,
> a member of the Magnificent Seven,
> the finest vintage wine,
> cooler than James Bond
> and hotter than Vesuvius.

- A simpler version is for children to stand up and declaim a boastful sentence, e.g.

  Child 1: I'm the person who can freeze fire.
  Child 2: So what? I'm the person who can catch clouds.
  Child 3: So what? I'm the person who can lift Everest.

THE EXQUISITE CORPSE (CONSEQUENCES)

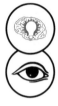

You will need: a piece of A4 paper for each child.

My family used to play 'Consequences' every Christmas. This activity is a version of the same game. It is called 'The exquisite corpse' after the first sentence obtained using the method by a group of Surrealists from the beginning of the last century:

> The exquisite corpse shall drink the new wine.

- Each child has a piece of paper. First of all they write down a determiner (a, the, some, those, this, that, etc.) at the top of the page. The paper is folded to hide the word and passed on.
- The second word is now written – this should be an adjective. Again the paper is folded to hide the word and passed on.
- Continue in this vein, writing the following word classes:

a determiner	(a)
an adjective	(shallow)
a noun	(starling)
a verb	(encourages)
an adverb	(carefully)
a preposition	(beside)
an adjective	(slow)
a noun	(rhyme)

- Sometimes the final results need a little tweaking, e.g.

> A shallow starling was encouraged carefully beside the slow rhyme.

SENSES TRAIL

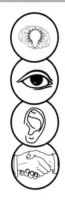

This is a multi-sensory game designed to help children observe the details of their surroundings. Try using it before focusing on 'settings' in narrative writing.

Take children outside with mini-whiteboards or notebooks. They should collect ideas and words under sense headings – sight, sound, taste, touch, smell. Use the notes as a basis for a list poem of likes/dislikes, e.g.

I like to see . . .
the red buses lumbering down Downsell
    Road,
sunlight striking the tower block's window
    panes,
the ducks bobbing for bread on the pond,
snow on my window when I open my
    curtains . . .

I don't like to see . . .
an endless traffic jam when I'm late for
    football,
lorries bullying their way up the avenue,
    belching smoke,
a lost child crying,
the look on my Dad's face when he sees the
    broken window . . .

QUESTION AND ANSWER

You will need: a piece of A4 paper for each child.

This is played in a similar way to 'Consequences', by writing and folding over a piece of paper to hide what has been written.

- In pairs, the first player writes a question on a piece of paper, folds it over then passes the sheet to the second child. The partner provides an answer. Obviously these will not match, but may provide some interesting chimes.
- As always, begin by doing some together as a class. You may want to help the children by suggesting what the questions might be about. For starters, list on a board some key question words, e.g.

  Who
  Where
  When
  Why
  What
  How
  Is . . .?
  Does . . .?
  Do . . .?
  Are . . .?
  Can . . .?
  Will . . .?

- Then make a list of subjects about which questions might be asked. Questions could be asked about any of the following – a tree, car, cat, cloud, moon, sun, lock, key, pool, forest, tower, flame, snowflake, crust, atom, ant, wolf, spider, eye, etc. So, a question might be 'Are oak trees meant to live forever?'

- When playing the game, the partner will not know what the question is. To come up with an answer they should take the list of subjects – or anything else they can think of – and provide an answer about that, starting with either 'yes' or 'no', e.g. 'No, wolves are not found in Scotland.'
- Now look at the question and the answer together, e.g.

> Q: Are oak trees meant to live forever?
> A: No, wolves are not found in Scotland.

CONDITIONALS

You will need: a piece of A4 paper for each child.

This game is similar to the 'Question and answer' game above, only this time the pairs have to write conditional sentences together.

- The first player writes an opening hypothetical clause beginning with 'if' or 'when', e.g. 'If the world was made of custard' or 'When the clocks strike twelve'.
- This is hidden by folding the paper over before being passed to the second child. The partner chooses a subject and writes a sentence in the conditional or future tense – using the words 'would', 'should' 'will' or 'could', e.g. 'a fox would tunnel deep' or 'the pudding will be well cooked'. Each child writes in a different colour so that their contributions stand out from one another.
- When they have written three or four sentences they should unravel the paper and take a look! Their sentences might read something like this:

If the world was made of custard,
a fox would tunnel deep.

When the clocks strike twelve,
the pudding will be well cooked.

- Another alternative is for everyone to write five questions followed by five 'if' or 'when' openings and then five endings. These can then be swapped over and matched with other classmates' suggestions. The results can be quite startling, e.g.

If there were no swans,
The snow would cover the porch.

If leopards lost their spots,
The match would have to be postponed.

When the wind blows from the North,
The pane of glass will break.

When the traffic lights turn green,
Father Christmas will refuse to visit.

SYLLOGISMS

You will need: a piece of A4 paper for each child.

A syllogism is a form of logical reasoning that consists of two premises and a conclusion. This idea was adopted by the Surrealists and turned into a writing game. It provides an interesting structure for writing that often leads to striking results.

The game is similar to 'Conditionals', but groups of three are needed.

- Player one writes down a proposition beginning with the word 'all', e.g. 'All eagles have two wings'. You may need to prompt sentences by listing possible topics, e.g. traffic jams, eagles, dogs, schools, milk, clouds, stars, flowers, squares, triangles, bread, wheat, Egypt, Africa, sunlight, dust, etc. When they have finished, the paper is folded over and passed to Player two.
- The second player writes down a further proposition, starting with the word 'there'. This needs to be about a different topic, e.g. 'There are only three corners to a triangle'. The paper is then folded over a second time and passed to Player three.
- The third player writes a conclusion – again, about a new topic – beginning with the word 'therefore', e.g. 'Therefore the wind is very cold'.
- Only when all three sentences have been written can the paper be unfolded. The sentences may need some adjustment and should be read aloud, e.g.

> All eagles have two wings.
> There are only three corners to a triangle.
> Therefore the wind is very cold.

> All clouds are damp.
> There are no orchids on the moon.
> Therefore the car will not start.

This is another game that was popular with the Surrealists because it depended on chance. Random ideas might produce something that was original – startling and occasionally beautiful. Young children enjoy the unique and unusual mixtures that can arise. This sort of game helps to break down inhibitions and open up the possibilities – as if words were pawns that could be shifted around to create all sorts of combinations.

OPPOSITES (1)

You will need: a sheet of A4 paper for each child.

This is another game that is related to 'Consequences'. This time the children work in pairs to write sentences that are opposite to each other. The exercise isn't as easy as it may sound – it demands some flexibility. If opposites are difficult to come up with, something close will do – near enough is better than nothing at all! Practise some together until the children get the hang of it.

- The first player writes down a statement, e.g.

  The old goat eats fresh grass.

- The next player looks at this and writes down the opposite, e.g.

  The young camel swallows stale soap.

- Next, the paper is folded down to hide the first line. The first player then writes the opposite to the second line, e.g.

  The ancient crow chews new iron bars.

- The paper is folded down again to hide the second line. This continues until there is no more room left to write.

OPPOSITES (2)

This is a simpler version of the previous game and is a great way to get children thinking about everyday things in new and imaginative ways. Adrian Henri's poem 'Tonight at Noon' is based on a title from a Charlie Mingus LP of the same name. In the poem he lists a series of opposite happenings. Use the same idea to create lists of opposites, e.g.

> <u>Tonight at noon</u>
> Rain will drip upwards,
> The sun will shine cold,
> Clocks will run backwards,
> Teachers will be set homework,
> Electric eels will get a nasty shock,
> Banks will open their vaults,
> And spelling tests will begin with the
>   answers . . .

CUT UPS (1)

You will need: exercise books, a set of recipe cards from a supermarket, a holiday brochure, newspapers and property advertisements, scissors (enough pairs for each child).

This game looks at what happens when you mix three or four different text types together.

- The children need to be in pairs for this game. Give each pair a recipe card, a page from the holiday brochure, newspaper and a property advertisement (you might want to enlarge this on a photocopier, depending on the size of the ad).
- The game is to cut out a sentence from each and then to slice the sentences into chunks. These

are then reassembled into new sentences using bits from different texts, e.g.

> Turn on the grill and ensuite bathroom complete with the sunniest climate in Europe and leave to toast for five minutes.

- Ensure that the children use the scissors correctly and safely. If you feel that the class can't cope sensibly with scissors, a good alternative is for the children to highlight the sentences they want to use and to list the 'chunks' in their exercise books. The new sentences can be assembled from this list, and written down.
- You can do the same sort of activity using any sort of text. For instance, children could work in pairs armed with any three books – a poetry collection, novel and textbook. Sentences could be constructed based on the rule that 'at least' two text types have to be involved in creating the sentence. Get them to write the sentences in their exercise books – chopping up books isn't allowed!
- Writing texts in different formats can also be very amusing. The easiest type to adapt is 'instructional' text. For instance, you could write instructions for a summer holiday in the style of a recipe, e.g.

> Take a sandy beach, blue sea, and hot sun. Stir in an ice-cream stall and leave to simmer . . .

- An amusing variant of this game is to 'subvert the genre'. Provide a short extract – say the start to a text – and the class have to continue the extract but radically alter the genre, e.g.

'I'll huff and I'll puff and I . . . love those curtains!'

Here we move from a traditional tale to 'Changing Rooms'!

CUT UPS (2)

You will need: short texts which need to be enlarged on a photocopier for cutting out (every child needs a copy of each text), scissors, a sheet of A4 paper for each child, glue.

Another fun way to play with cut ups is to pull apart then reassemble texts. Doing the activity in pairs can lead to some interesting discussions. Try the following method:

1. Select a short text – the sort of text that children are studying at the time, e.g. Roman lifestyle, volcanoes, life of a famous artist, etc.
2. Enlarge it on a photocopier so the font is fairly large (especially if you are going to use scissors for cutting up), then photocopy the text – one copy per child.
3. The next step is to cut it up. The text could be cut into paragraphs, sentences or even individual words. A poem could be cut up into verses or lines, with something like a haiku (see p. 91) being pulled apart word by word!
4. Now take a blank sheet of A4 paper and stick the bits of text down in a random order. Photocopy enough sheets for the class.
5. The children have to reassemble the cut-up text so that it makes sense.

Cutting the bits up and physically moving them round can make the task easier as it allows you to try out different combinations. However, if you feel that the class can't cope sensibly with scissors, a good alternative is for the children to rewrite the texts on a separate sheet of paper.

ALPHABETS

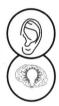

Alphabet games – of which there are many – make good warm-ups, not least because they emphasise an aspect of language that all children will need in everyday life – alphabetical order. Here are some tried-and-tested versions that have proved very popular with youngsters.

Version 1

The first game involves rapidly listing words within a given category, e.g. animals – one for each letter of the alphabet (or as many as possible), e.g.

ant
bear
cat
dog . . .

This can be extended by adding an adjective before the name of the animal and a verb after it – all starting with the same letter, e.g.

The adventurous ant ate
The bold bear blew
The curious cat caught
The dangerous dog dug . . .

Version 2

The second alphabet activity is based on 'The Minister's Cat' game, where adjectives starting with each letter of the alphabet are chosen to describe the Minister's Cat. Here you use a different owner and a different pet, e.g. 'The Teacher's Budgie' or 'The Teacher's Rottweiler', e.g.

> The Teacher's Earwig is
> An **a**ble Earwig
> A **b**rave Earwig . . .

Version 3

'Place alphabets' are a really great way to bring the alphabet alive. The children start off by choosing a place, e.g. the beach, town centre, playground, park, zoo, etc. They then make a list of what each letter did, e.g.

> At the zoo
> A **a**sked directions,
> B **b**uilt an aquarium,
> C **c**limbed with the monkeys . . .

Version 4

'Alphabets of ingredients' can be quite a fun way of playing with words and having to THINK hard:

* *An alphabet of treats* – here the children choose things that they love to do, e.g.

  > A was abseiling at the local sports centre.
  > B was buying an ice cream.
  > C was camping out under the stars.
  > D was driving a go-cart.

* *An alphabet of people* – in this alphabet the children choose a name and an object beginning with the same letter and think of an action to link the two, e.g.

Andrew built an **a**rk.
Billy ate a **b**anana.
Carrie sung like a **c**anary.

- *An alphabet of places* – use an atlas to make a list of places, trying to choose ones that have plenty of rhymes. These can be used to compose short jingles. The game makes a great paired activity, e.g.

  Found a four leaf clover
  Whilst in Andover.

  Found a baby's rattle
  In Battle.

  Found a smile
  In Carlisle.

  Found the sea
  While in Dundee.

ANIMAL COUNTING RHYMES

Counting and alliteration are the focus of this game. All that the children have to do is to write down ten things that different animals do.

- They should start by writing one to ten down the left-hand side of their mini-whiteboards.
- The next step is to think of an animal whose name begins with the first letter of the number, e.g. *one ostrich, two tigers* and so on.
- They then need to think of an action that the animal could be doing, also starting with the same letter, e.g. *one ostrich ogles*. A rhyme might start like this:

  One ostrich ogles,
  Two tigers talk,
  Three thrushes thirst,

Four frogs fight,
Five fish fly . . .

NURSERY RHYMES

You may find that you have to begin this jumpstart by reminding the children of some well-known nursery rhymes. The challenge in this game is to give traditional nursery rhymes a new twist!

Write a nursery rhyme on the whole-class board, e.g. Humpty Dumpty. The task is to rewrite it using the same structure and rhythm as the original, e.g.

Billy Bolly sat in the park
Billy Bolly had a great lark
All of those passing
And all the police
Couldn't help Billy to home again.

NEW DEFINITIONS

You will need: dictionaries.

The idea of this game is to create new definitions for different words. The activity helps children think about the true meaning of words. It stretches the youngsters' imaginations by encouraging them to look at things in new and unusual ways. This kind of suspension of belief can be quite liberating.

- Begin by listing random words for letters of the alphabet on the whole-class board. Next invent definitions – these can be as whacky as you like, e.g.

Art	– the place where dust settles in the night.
Branch	– a short catapult used by small boys.
Car	– the moment when the clocks stop.
Drag	– to watch clouds drift by . . .

- Alternatively, this can be played as a panel game. The panel members will need a dictionary. They choose an unfamiliar word (e.g. *shellac*) and provide either the correct definition, or an invented one. The class vote about whether they think the panel are lying or not. As a variation of this, the panel choose an unfamiliar word and provide three possible definitions, e.g.

    'Is a *shellac* (1) a rare seabird; (2) a silver coin that was used on the Isle of Man; or (3) resin used in varnishes?'

    The class have to decide which one is correct (in this case, it's the definition number 3).

SPOT THE LIAR

This is a quick and easy dictionary game that is guaranteed to appeal to youngsters. Children are both intrigued and excited by the idea of lying and tend to be well-versed at 'bending the truth'. Of course, in story writing the ability to fabricate is a must!

- Open a dictionary at random and select a word that everyone knows the meaning of, e.g. smoke. The children then have to write down a lie and a truth about the word, e.g.

Smoke is grey and the wind blows it easily.
Smoke is so heavy that not even a
champion tag wrestler could lift it up.

- Another game involves the children writing a
statement about themselves in each corner of
their mini-whiteboard. Three should be true
and one a lie. They should then share these in
pairs – can their partner guess the untruth?

PICK AND MIX

You will need: a photocopied sheet containing a list
of words (suggested list given below) (one copy per
child).

This game introduces children to Haiku – a
Japanese form of poetry which is thought to have a
strict syllabic content but is actually quite flexible.

- Before the session begins prepare a list of words
for the children to use. Draw a container on a
sheet of paper (e.g. a bag, a box, a treasure
chest, etc.). Write a variety of words inside the
container – include nouns, adjectives, verbs and
adverbs. Photocopy the sheet and give one to
each child. The task is for each of them to:

  1. Select a given number of words (let's say
  five).
  2. Write a haiku – two or three lines long
  (don't worry about counting syllables for
  the haiku – two or three lines will be
  sufficient as a guideline).
  3. All five words have to be used – though
  verbs may be adapted, nouns pluralised,
  etc. to help the sense.

4. You could ask the children to include a
   particular feature, e.g. a simile, metaphor,
   personification or alliteration.

- Begin by demonstrating a class version. Ask the
  children to select five words, e.g. 'cheek',
  'perch', 'glare', 'egg', 'edge'. Then try to work
  the given words into a two- or three-line
  snapshot, e.g.

  The egg's frail cheek
  Perched on the edge
  Of the clown's glare.

- Don't worry if the end result is somewhat
  surreal. The game is about beginning to tussle
  with language.

Some suggested words to use (or choose your own)
Moon print silk red kindle glass sharp sun mirror
edge perfect shape cut night scarlet beak window
door peak glare sullen jagged donkey clip raid
grasp apple guide knife attic teeth green mild
wind dig rain shot bees lock finger tip cheek dusk
bloom perch glue blind eyes fidget yawn restless
taxis shuffle bruise knuckle punch melt spin fire
roar holler slip smooth egg blue velvet dark silver
stars clouds glass sharp grass wet silk shot trees
arch curve edge silent sky time cat the a hill car
street flame scraps ragged tongue lips eyes
glares stares glances runs sleeps curls yellow
spills crush ice cut hands skin black leaves
certain sudden unease captivate imprison trap
cage start release first heart fool hero stumble
part meet greet tower buzz fly seek grow shrivel
jailor guards

BOX OF WORDS

You will need: a piece of A4 paper for each child, an empty box or bag, a visual stimulus (e.g. a picture, photo, video clip, etc.).

This is another version of the 'Pick and mix' game, in which children generate words, images and ideas from a visual stimulus.

- Start with an empty box or bag (this will be filled with words, images and ideas). Show the box to the class and put it to one side.
- A starting point is needed – any clear image will do, but preferably something tangible that can be seen, e.g. a tower, a river, the night sky, a face, a bicycle, a fire, an explosion, etc. Many children find it easier if you bring the list alive by using a real object (e.g. a key, a candle, etc.) or an image – photos, postcards, posters, slides and video clips are all helpful. Make sure that you select one clear and striking image.
- Now the box has to be filled with similes. Ask the class what the subject is 'like' – what it reminds them of, what it looks like. Provide a few examples to get them going. If, for instance, you chose the night sky as your image, you could give the following simile as an example:

    Stars are like tin tacks.

    Accept everything – even the more bizarre – and fill the box or bag. The ideas might then be strung together to form a sort of riddle based on a cairn of similes, e.g.

What am I?
Like –
a red cut,
a thin leaf of tissue paper,
a dark eye set in a scarlet face,
a blood orange,
a torn Chinese lantern . . .

(Answer = a poppy)

- Another strategy is to select one simile and then extend the idea, e.g.

Stars are like tin tacks
Glittering in the darkness,
Holding up the dark cloth of night,
Pinning it back,
Their sharp barbs digging
Into the soft black skin above . . .

INQUISITIVE BOXES

You will need: a large cardboard box containing a variety of objects that can be used to jumpstart talk and writing (suggested list given below).

Years ago I was told by somebody that an 'interest box' was an essential part of the teacher's toolkit. Mine is an 'inquisitive box'. A large cardboard box is ideal, in which can be stored all sorts of odd curios. Build up your collection over time. My box holds, among other things: a feather, a tiny shoe, a ship in a bottle, an old key, an old map, an unusual piece of bark, a leaf skeleton, a miniature box with a unicorn on the lid, an old pen with a golden nib, a tiny red dragon, a large magnifying glass, a badger's skull, a glass jar of buttons, and an assortment of coins from different countries.

Items can be removed from the box and used in different ways to jumpstart talk or writing.

- One by one, volunteers choose an object (something different each time) and the children each write a description of the item on their mini-whiteboard. Alternatively, use it as a starting point for a story. For instance, the buttons could be given out and questions asked to build the tale, e.g.

  What garment did your button come off?
  Who last wore the garment?
  Where were they when they lost the button?
  What were they doing?
  Was anyone else there?
  What had just happened to the character?
  Where did they go?
  When did they notice the button had gone?
  What was their reaction?
  Who picked it up?
  What did they do with it?

- Having discussed the background to the story, children could enact some of these scenes, improvising in pairs. This is a great way to lead into planning and writing a story.

PHILIP GROSS JUMPSTARTS A WRITING WORKSHOP

In the late 1980s, poet and novelist Philip Gross wrote an excellent poetry book, *Manifold Manor* (Faber & Faber 1989), which is a serious poetry game itself – and should be part of every teacher's poetry kit. The book acts as an invitation to write. I asked Philip if he had a few activities that might help to warm up creative thinking and this is what he wrote back:

I'm sure I use the same few families of games and tricks that all of us do, just working our own small folk-art variations in the telling, and with particular personal intents. For example . . .

Word associations ... and disassociations
A few rounds of word associations, getting quicker and more willing to trust whatever comes. The message: don't think hard; think soft and light. Spot and trust the first thought, the one that comes quicker than you can check it or test it to see if you think that's what the teacher wants. A game in which there are no right and no wrong answers; what matters is the flow.

THEN when it starts to feel easy, try a few rounds in which there must be no associations whatsoever – not by meaning or by sound. (Spell out what some of the sound-associations might be: alliteration, rhyme, etc.). After a first round, ask everyone in the group to watch for possible associations – put up a hand if you think you spot one. The message: human brains are natural association machines. Just let them do their job and they'll give you new ideas, AND the sound-play that makes for poetry. Learning terms like 'rhyme', 'alliteration', 'assonance', etc. only teaches us to name what our ears and brain do spontaneously (if we don't stop them).

Disregarded things

It's never true that 'there's nothing to write about'. The world is absolutely full of things . . . most of which we ignore. The instruction is: look round the room you're in – the more ordinary the better – and think this: somewhere in this room is one tiny detail that nobody has ever noticed before (e.g. that piece of Blu-tack, that crack in the ceiling, that dead fly in the light fitment, etc.). Look round and trust that one will call out to you: it needs you. There may be several, but choose the one that seems the most small, slight, unexpected and unregarded. Then go round in a circle, and each person speaks up for their thing – giving it words, saying 'I' not 'it', saying what it feels like being it.

This can be a quick-fire starter, simply raising everyone's attention to detail, but can also be the start of poems: an astonishing range of feelings find themselves invested in neglected details.

The point, in the end, is how our games are played in the live situation; for a leader/teacher with a feel for poetry, anything becomes an opportunity. With no feel, the best exercise can be a chore.

Philip's other poetry books for young writers are Scratch City *(1995) and* The All-Nite Cafe *(1993) which won the Signal Award in 1974 (both published by Faber & Faber). His most recent novel is* Going for Stone *(Oxford University Press 2002).*

LINDA NEWBERY ON FAVOURITE WORDS

The novelist Linda Newbery has several ways into starting writing workshops. As she told me in a recent email:

When working with a new group, especially when the children don't know each other, I tell them about some favourite words of mine and ask them to choose one favourite word each. So I might start with 'dishevelled' or 'wobble' (depending on the age of the group) and explain why I like that word. We then go round the group, treating it as a memory game, connecting each word with the chooser's own name. Sometimes, the chosen word becomes the chooser's nickname for the day or the weekend.

This can be extended, if wished, to an oral group story in which all the chosen words must be used.

I usually make sure I begin a workshop with an idea everyone can cope with, e.g. 'Sad I Ams' (e.g. 'I am sad when I see a dog limping', 'I am sad when I am not allowed to stay up late', etc.) or some other list poem, or a simple group kenning* poem. I often like to make a group poem using one line from everyone, e.g. iambic pentameters (for fairly able children) in which each line starts with 'I wish . . .', e.g. 'I wish I had a slice of cherry cake'.

* A compoound expression used in Old English and Norse poetry which names something without using its name, e.g. mouse-catcher (cat)

Do check out Linda's books, BLITZ BOYS (A & C Black 2001) and the Moving On trilogy – No Way Back (2001), Break Time (2002) and Windfall (2002) from Orchard Books. Contact with Linda for school visits can be made through Jan or Ellie Powling at Speaking of Books, jan@speakingofbooks .co.uk. Speaking of Books runs an excellent service for booking authors/poets. They deal with all arrangements and provide a unique service.

JAMES CARTER'S POETRY JUMPSTARTS

 The poet James Carter uses this idea as a jumpstart to some of his poetry workshops. He writes up on a board the title of the first chapter plus the opening line from J. K. Rowling's first Harry Potter novel, *Harry Potter and the Philosopher's Stone* (Bloomsbury 1997).

> The Boy Who Lived
>
> Mr and Mrs Dursley, of number four, Privet Drive, were proud to say that they were perfectly normal, thank you very much.

The children then have two minutes to rearrange the lines as if it was a poem. Ask one or two of them to do this straight onto an OHP, or to type it into an interactive whiteboard or PC. These versions can be used for discussion.

As James told me in a recent email:

> My model – of course, it could be done in a whole myriad of ways – is like this:
>
> **The Boy Who Lived**
>
> Mr and Mrs (*nice alliterative phrase*)
> Dursley (*highlights what a wonderfully horrible name it is!*)
> of number four
> Privet Drive
> were proud
>   to say (*internal rhyme with 'they'!*)
>   that they (*more alliteration!*)
> were yltcefrep ʅɐɯɹou (*perfectly is backwards (imperfectly) and 'normal' written upside down*)
>
> thank
>   you
>   very
>   much.

I tell children there is no wrong way of doing it – and some end up rearranging the lines as a shape poem – some as a magic wand, wizard's hat, a road map, Harry's zigzag scar, a number four, etc. I stress that short lines work best, as they allow the reader to enjoy and focus on every word. I have taken the punctuation out, but it can be left in. Children always ask if they can add or take away words, but I don't allow it!

James's poetry book Cars, Stars, Electric Guitars *(Walker Books 2002) provides many simple models. Also look at his* Creating Writers: a Creative Writing Manual for Schools *(RoutledgeFalmer 2000) and* Just Imagine: Creative Ideas for Writing *(David Fulton Publishers 2002). For writing workshops and INSET courses contact James at: 94 Halfpenny Cottages, Papist Way, Cholsey, Oxon. OX10 9QJ.*

LUNCHTIME

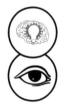

James's game can also be played the other way round. Choose a short poem that you like. Write it out as if it was prose – the children then have to rewrite it on their mini-whiteboards, deciding where the line breaks should be. Try using my poem 'Lunchtime' (p. 102). There are, of course, many ways it could be set out (the children needn't stick to my layout), but the prose version would look something like this:

The boys lay claim to the playground, staking out their territory with sweaters. They whoop and yell, punching the air as if they were stars on 'Match of the Day'. The girls huddle to one side, clapping rhythms, skipping rhymes, hop-scotching their time. Dinner ladies, like Sumo wrestlers, stand guard. The Infants steer clear and wonder when their Mums will come to take them home. A lone teacher hugs her coffee mug, shrugs off the wind, and casts a watchful eye. Other kids gather in corners to swap bubblegum cards and jokes they don't understand.

LUNCHTIME

The boys lay claim
to the playground,
staking out their territory
with sweaters.
They whoop and yell,
punching the air
as if they were stars
on 'Match of the Day'.

The girls huddle to one side,
clapping rhythms,
skipping rhymes,
hop-scotching their time.

Dinner ladies,
like Sumo wrestlers,
stand guard.

The Infants steer clear
and wonder when
their Mums will come
to take them home.

A lone teacher hugs
her coffee mug,
shrugs off the wind,
and casts a watchful eye.

Other kids gather in corners
to swap bubblegum cards
and jokes
they don't
understand.

Pie Corbett

MINI SAGAS

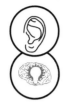

You will need: exercise books, a book of nursery rhymes, a collection of fairy tales, a narrative poem of your choice.

You don't have to look too far to find inspiration for mini sagas. These are great fun to write and are a terrific way for children to practise identifying and summarising the main points of a text.

Begin by asking the children to write a mini saga of around 50 words telling the tale of a nursery rhyme. The advantage of a rhyme is that the children know the story already, e.g.

> Humpty had promised his mum
> to take care, but that afternoon he
> went up to the wall and sat there
> with his legs dangling. Unfortunately,
> the wind blew a mighty gust and
> he fell. The king's soldiers tried
> to save him but the mess was
> only good for scrambled egg!

- Most rhymes may need some extra detail added to them. However, move on to rewriting fairy tales as mini sagas and they will need to trim the tale back to its bare bones, e.g.

> Red walked to her Granny's.
> Unfortunately, a wolf followed
> her. The wolf got there first and
> killed Granny. It put on her
> clothes and tried to fool Red
> by mimicking Granny. It was
> about to eat Red, when a
> woodcutter, who had seen
> the wolf, dashed in and killed it.

- As an extension to these activities see if the children can rewrite a narrative poem as a 50-word telegram.

KATHERINE GALLAGHER'S WORD WARM-UPS

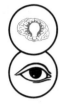

The poet Katherine Gallagher has some interesting ways into starting her writing workshops. In a recent email, she described some of these to me:

I use these to help the group feel at ease with the writing activity – with themselves and me. Following from this, I want them to feel the particular exercise is fun and that they can let their imaginations zoom.

1. When doing 'Food' as a topic, it's good to start them off with Ogden Nash's poem, 'Mustard', in which he writes about food that he is 'mad about'. I then ask the class, 'WHAT ARE YOU MAD ABOUT?' They usually begin with serious replies such as 'hamburger and chips', but with some encouragement I take the idea into the surreal. After an exchange of surreal ideas, I ask them to do a list poem starting, *I'm mad about* . . .

2. Another idea is to get them to brainstorm on the subject, 'If I were a vegetable'. Warm them up with a couple of vegetable poems, e.g. 'The Cabbage is a Funny Veg.' by Roger McGough (from *A Catalogue of Comic Verse*, selected by Rolf Harris, Hodder Children's Books 1988). Get them to write, 'If I were a vegetable, I'd . . .' The same can be applied to fruit. As a starter, these could be simple but effective. One student, Aron Fallon, wrote:

> If I were a fruit,
> I would be a tomato
> and would get
> crunched
> by clean
> teeth.

Both of these starters produce amazing, amusing poems. Since the above exercises involve students' own responses, these questions can be adapted to almost every topic under the sun.

3. Start off by saying, 'You know, giants always get very hungry. What sort of food do they eat?' The students' replies will range from the absurd to the ordinary. When I do this I then say, 'Here's what they like for a special treat' and I read 'Giants' Delight' by Steven Kroll (from *A Catalogue of Comic Verse*). I get them to repeat this after me. They love to chant it and it gets them in the mood to start writing their own 'Giant's Delight'. This exercise can be varied, e.g. 'What do Prime Ministers, Queens, Burglars or Wrestlers eat?'

4. Another idea to get them writing is the theme of favourite places. Brainstorm a few landmarks (maybe local), not necessarily tourist places but sites that are important/ familiar to them. Then ask them if they know Dot Hog's hot-dog stand. I read Kit Wright's 'Fast Food' poem, which is all about Dot Hog (from his collection *Cat Among the Pigeons*, Puffin Books 1989). I've found that repeating the poem helps them to get into the mood for writing – they like the tongue-twister aspect and the speed. Get them to write a few alliterative lines about their favourite place.

5. Another idea is 'BUNGEE-JUMPING WITH WORDS' – an exercise in using similes and metaphors. List with the children some everyday objects, e.g. house, computer, garden, piano, shoe. Then after brainstorming, do a whole-class poem on the board where the children contribute, e.g.

    Piano
    –   is a row of teeth
    –   is a book of songs
    –   is a polished house on wheels . . .

These bungee-jumping exercises usually become increasingly wide-ranging/absurd, are fun and endlessly diverting.

6. Any subject that allows children to call on their knowledge and individual experience usually works best. Some starter lines are suggested by Richard Edwards's poem 'Finding out about the Family' (from his collection *Teaching the Parrot*, Faber & Faber 1997). Examples of lead lines include: 'It was really rather scary . . .', 'It was really rather odd . . .', 'It was most bizarre of all . . .'

I hope the above is useful. I think the great secret of poetry is to be 'freefall', ready to 'go with the flow', as tutor or teacher.

For school visits, Katherine can be contacted at: 49 Myddleton Road, London N22 8LZ. Telephone 0208 881 1418 or email Katherine_Gallagher@compuserve.com. Her website is: http:// ourworld.compuserve.com/homepages/katherine_gallagher

CRAZY WRITING

This is an opportunity to write rapidly and loosen up the mind. By 'crazy' I mean that it doesn't really matter if the children play with ideas in a surreal manner, inventing verbal jokes along the way. Of course – they love it!

• Read out a crazy list like the one below.

I wish I was the beat of bumble bee's flight.
I wish I was the shadow of an ant's back leg.
I wish I was the hum of a guitar string strummed.
I wish I was an antique fan fluttering like an eyelid.

I wish I was a newspaper cutting . . . your
mind with sharp words.
I wish I was a bus station trembling in the
heat haze.
I wish I was a lamp post stooping down to
tickle a car's chin.
I wish I was a tower block yawning last
thing at night.
I wish I was a coffee cup whistling a sneaky
tune.
I wish I was an old goat's beard, dripping
with wisdom.
I wish I was a chocolate flame.
I wish I was the first word that was ever
spoken.
I wish I was the last thought that you had,
as you heard these words fly like birds
from the page.

Invent a few crazy ideas as a whole class. Then give
the children three minutes to write as many crazy
ideas as possible – the idea is to write at speed.
Sense doesn't matter too much, as these are crazy
ideas.

Occasionally, I have known children come up with
some of their finest writing during this sort of
activity. It is as if the normal conditions for writing
are not always conducive to genuine creativity. It
also occurs to me that letting go of logical thought
and just following your instinctive inventiveness
may be what writers need to do when they are
creating – letting go and trusting that inner
intelligence. Try it and see!

EXPRESSIONS

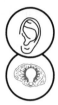

This game relies on taking a fresh look at everyday sayings that we use but barely think about. It helps us consider language anew and probes deep into the metaphorical use of expressions.

- Make a class collection of everyday expressions, e.g.

  > Play by ear
  > Box your ears
  > It's raining cats and dogs
  > It's a crying shame
  > That's a piece of cake
  > She'll hit the roof
  > Her eyes shot across the room
  > I've caught a cold
  > She's got her head in the clouds
  > She has a heart of stone
  > Has the cat got your tongue?

- These can be listed on the whole-class board and used in various ways. For instance, children could work in pairs to decide on the story that leads to one of the expressions. They may need several minutes to work the story out.
- A fun alternative is to try using the expressions and taking them literally. Children could be asked to write two or three lines for each expression. These poetic fragments might look something like this:

  > She slammed the door in my face –
  > But when she had gone,
  > I carefully opened it.

  > I caught a cold
  > Stealing from the freezer!

  > She said it was a piece of cake
  > So I ate it up . . .

'The poem imagines it is a horror film' (see below) is based on more ghoulish expressions! You might like to share it with the children before they make a start on their own 'literal lines'. But be warned . . . doing so could have gruesome consequences!

THE POEM IMAGINES IT IS A HORROR FILM

He was so afraid that
He had his heart in his mouth.
(Bloodstains covered his tie.)

It was so funny that
She laughed her head off.
(They couldn't stitch it back on.)

'Don't look a gift horse in the mouth,'
I was told at school.
(They bite.)

I hit the nail on the head.
(It screamed with pain.)

I was so angry
That it made my blood boil.
(My brains cooked nicely.)

When she lied
I saw right through her.
(The hole in her head bled.)

My heart sank into my boots.
(The blood warmed my feet.)

It's not fair –
My teacher keeps
Jumping down my throat.
(It makes it hard to breeeeeeeathe.)

Pie Corbett

MESSAGES

You will need: an enlarged version of 'Message for the mice that live in the roof' (see opposite), or enough copies of it for each child.

My family love leaving messages. They use post-it notes and love to stick them in unusual places – inside my shoes, on a pillow, in the fridge, on a chair and so on. The idea of leaving messages can lead to some quick-fire fun that stimulates the imagination.

- As a group, talk about what message you would leave for different animals or objects, e.g. the cat, a mouse, a dog, a fly, a mosquito, an ant army, a pillow, a shoe, a staircase, an oven, a teapot, a TV, etc.
- Stick the enlarged version of 'Message for the mice that live in the roof' to the whole-class board, or hand out photocopies to each child. It's a message I wrote for the not-so-welcome housemates in my roof!

**MESSAGE FOR THE MICE THAT
LIVE IN THE ROOF**

I've left you a present.
It's all I could find –
just a chunk of sweaty cheddar
that had gone hard,
and some cold bacon rind.
Sorry but –
there was nothing classier
in the fridge,
and I didn't think
that you'd care
for scraps of garlic.
(I've left the cheese
on the red dish
by the cat
flap.)

Pie Corbett

- Ideally, messages should be put onto post-it notes and placed on a message board. It might be fun to write some secret messages with one object writing to another. What would the toaster say to the teapot?
- You could also leave messages for fairy tale characters:

  Dear Jack – thanks for leaving me the goose. It tasted excellent. I am looking forward to hearing about this new way you have discovered of making money, love – Jill.

LISTS

You will need: sheets of A4 paper or exercise books.

Lists are very liberating and make excellent warm-ups for writing. These could be about almost anything (as the following LIST shows!):

> Shiny things
> Soft things
> Quiet things
> Noisy things
> Places I love
> What is happening now
> Places I've visited
> Things I like doing
> 5 things in an emu's beak
> 5 things inside the Queen's handbag .
> 5 things in a giant's cave
> 5 things in an Ofsted inspector's case . . .

Here are two of my own lists to give you an idea of what the children should be aiming for.

> <u>Six things found in an elf's backpack</u>
> A bee's sting for giving bullies a sudden
>   shock.
> A tooth, that looks like a fresh-water pearl,
>   stolen from under a child's pillow.
> A floppy hat made from a purple foxglove.
> An old grey hair snatched from a goat's
>   beard, to be used for tickling a teacher's
>   nose.
> A well-thumbed encyclopaedia of trickery.
> A bag of never-ending wishes.

<u>Six things found in a goblin's sack</u>
A nightmare, made from a clap of thunder,
    ready to be tipped into a sleeping
    parent's ear.
The two ends stolen from a rainbow.
A whip of lightning for lashing those caught
    out in a storm.
An umbrella made out of a red cap fungus.
A pack of cards with a lie written on each
    one.
A bag of wind.

'Things to do at a birthday party' shows how lists can be set out in lots of different ways. Once the children have written their lists, see if they can design an interesting and relevant layout on the page.

THINGS TO DO AT A BIRTHDAY PARTY

Wait up late
    the night before
        unable to sleep
            shadows shifting in the
              darkened bedroom

Run from room to room
    screaming like a banshee
        pin up birthday cards
            hide a five pound note
            away

Wonder who Uncle George might be
    tie balloons to the gate
        peer down the street
            wait for your friends
              stomach in a knot

Screw up wrapping paper into a massive
  ball
      kick it round the room
        score a few goals
           make a cairn of presents

Watch a frightening film
    greedily eat sweet popcorn
        go ice skating
            listen to the quick, slick
            hiss of skates

Blow out candles on a cake
    watch another year dash past
                Pie Corbett

CHAPTER 5

Jumpstarting speaking, listening and drama

All these games involve children in speaking and listening. Many would make good warm-ups for drama, but are just as useful as a lively way into reading or writing sessions. They typically demand full participation, concentration and the use of the imagination to enter the world of the drama. Often they test the children's ability to think rapidly on their feet, inventing as they go along. Nearly all have an element of paired or group work and get the children used to articulating their ideas and feelings, or dramatically creating a role. Talking can be a helpful precursor to writing as it allows children the chance to rehearse ideas. Some of the games are also forms of dramatic comprehension which demand that the children imaginatively enter the world of the story that is being studied.

JUST A MINUTE

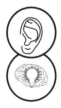

You will need: a container (e.g. a box, tin, bag, hat, etc.), small cut up pieces of paper.

This could be used as a precursor to a topic – to see what is generally known, or just after it – to gauge levels of understanding. Alternatively, it could be used just for fun – to see who can talk on any topic without hesitation, repetition or deviation. Either way it's a great opportunity for children to practise speaking audibly, clearly and with confidence, and it is also useful for reinforcing turn-taking skills.

- Ask the children to write possible topics on a piece of paper. Put them in a container (a hat, a box, etc.) and then select at random!
- Tell them that they will have a minute to talk on the topic they've chosen, during which time they must not hesitate, repeat or deviate otherwise they are out of the game.
- Taking a few minutes to rehearse in pairs can be helpful – if any of the children get stuck, their partners can make suggestions relevant to the topic.

ANIMAL, VEGETABLE OR MINERAL

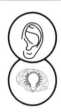

This is a fun game that encourages participants to ask relevant and appropriate questions to clarify understanding.

- A volunteer comes into the 'hot seat' and thinks of an object or thing. The person tells the class whether it is animal, vegetable or mineral.
- The class ask questions to which the answer can only be 'yes', 'no' or 'maybe'. Can they guess what the mystery thing is within 20 questions?

DO EXACTLY AS I SAY

The focus of this activity is on choosing the precise words needed to persuade someone to carry out an action. As well as exploring the best ways to persuade and explain things to others, the children also have to think about the order in which they give instructions.

- One child takes off a pullover or coat. The others take it in turns to give an instruction which the listener must follow literally. The aim of the game is to get the volunteer to put the item of clothing back on – not as easy as it sounds! For instance, an instruction to 'put your arm into the sleeve' might lead to a left arm being placed in a right-hand sleeve so the coat is on back to front!
- Explain to the children that their instructions need to be as specific as possible, e.g. 'Turn the jumper round so that the hole for the head is at the top' and so on.
- A simpler version of this game is to try to get someone to move from their seat to the class door.

GOOD MORNING, YOUR MAJESTY

You will need: a blindfold (e.g. a scarf or similar piece of material).

This game is very handy for those odd five-minute slots that occasionally appear, or as a warm-up for a drama session. It involves being able to listen very carefully. Children love it!

A volunteer sits in the 'hot seat' and is blindfolded. The teacher points to someone else, who creeps up to the person sitting in the 'hot seat' and disguises their voice to say, 'Good morning, your Majesty'. The blindfolded person has to guess who it is. They swap over when the blindfolded person guesses incorrectly.

MIRRORS

This game makes a very useful warm-up for drama. It involves concentrating, imitating and working closely with a partner.

Both children face each other. One leads and the other follows. The follower is the mirror and has to perfectly copy the leader's body movements and facial expression. After a few minutes, they swap over.

ANECDOTES

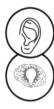

In this game the children share anecdotes. The exercise gives them the chance to speak confidently about a topic of their choice. We are all experts on our own experience. This can act as a potent source for talk.

- It can be handy to begin such a 'recount' session by telling a few anecdotes of your own – choose interesting and unusual experiences that will appeal to the children. These could be based around three topics:

  1. Places – best and worst, dreadful holidays, secret hiding places, etc.
  2. People – weird, unusual, most frightening, old relatives, etc.
  3. Events – most memorable, favourite and worst, moving home, etc.

- Ask the children to tell their anecdotes to one another in pairs. Then swap partners. This provides a chance to retell the original anecdote, or to retell their friend's.
- You can now pause and talk about how the second telling might be orally revised – maybe using a sharper opening or clearer ending? Anecdoting is an excellent way into writing short recounts or narratives.
- An extension of this is for children to take the role of a character from a fairytale and to come up with an anecdote that tells their story.

WALKING

Try this game as another way to begin a drama session, or when moving into writing about character. It concerns adopting the character or 'mantle' of another person or creature and thinking carefully about how movement reflects or suggests personality.

- Divide the class into small groups and give each one an instruction to walk in a certain way, e.g. 'like an animal', 'like someone who's lost', 'as though you're upset', ' like a King' and so on.
- Explain that each group in turn is going to wander about in a walk appropriate to the instruction they have just been given, e.g. like a monkey, backwards and forwards looking confused, head hung low and shoulders hunched, majestically, etc. The other children must guess what the group is trying to show.
- An alternative exercise is for one person to walk round the room with a slight exaggeration, e.g. raising and lowering a shoulder. A second child joins behind and exaggerates further, e.g. lifting one arm up and down. A third joins in and

exaggerates even more, e.g. swinging both arms from side to side. Try to give the children as much space as possible to do this in – playing it in the hall or playground is best.

IMPOSSIBLE ACTIONS

When I was a child we spent hours trying to pat our head with one hand and rub our tummy with the other. This game is a version of that. It makes a good warm-up as it involves concentration and trying to make the brain do two very distinctly different actions at once! This would be handy in drama, but don't be afraid to try these games at the start of other sessions as a way of firing up the brain and tuning the class into concentrating.

Challenge the children to draw a cross with one hand and a circle with the other simultaneously on their mini-whiteboards. When they have finished get them to swap hands and try again!

PASS A RHYTHM

This whole-class activity is a handy way to tune children into concentrating and listening carefully. Some storytellers use this sort of game at the start of a session, just to engage everyone's close attention.

Sit with the children in a circle. Explain to the group that you are going to clap a simple rhythm which you'd like them to take it in turns to repeat. The rhythm is clapped and passed rapidly round the room. When it gets back to you, choose another person to start the group off with another simple rhythm.

PARTY GAME

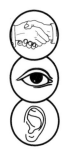

This mime-based activity is a real favourite with adults and children alike. Participants take it in turns to guess the roles of other group members simply by watching them mime. No verbal clues or questioning are allowed – it's very challenging and very exciting!

- Divide the children into groups of four. One person plays the party host while the other three take the role of guests.
- Each guest chooses a role (e.g. ballerina, secret agent, someone scared of tables, etc.) and is welcomed into the party. The guest then mimes the person they have chosen to be and the host has to guess who they are.
- Keep reminding the children that miming doesn't involve speaking. Encourage them to think carefully about their movements, gestures and facial expression.

MONOLOGUES AND DUOLOGUES

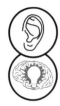

You will need: photocopies of the poem 'The Wolf's wife speaks' (pp. 123 and 124) (enough for each child).

This activity is a great confidence builder and is designed to give all children a chance to make a contribution in drama sessions. It works well because children are great at chatting – and that is the main skill needed!

- Use 'The Wolf's wife speaks' as a monologue to be learned and/or performed, or as a duologue with two children taking alternate verses. Encourage the children to put lots of expression into it. See if they can vary their tone, gestures and facial expression depending on what they are saying. They should also think about pace (which bits are slow or quick), where to leave pauses, changing volume (loud, soft, whispered), using expression (angry, sad, etc.). Effective speaking aloud involves varying how you speak in relation to the meaning. So – think 'vary it'!
- Alternatively, ask the children to choose a traditional tale that they know well. Get them to think about minor characters, or to invent characters who do not appear in the actual tale. In pairs, they should 'gossip' or 'think aloud' about what has happened in the story.

THE WOLF'S WIFE SPEAKS

He was always out and about.
First on the block
To be up at the crack of dawn
Sniffing the morning air.

Of course,
Pork was his favourite.
I tell you, he would go a long way
For a nice bit of crackling,
Or to catch a tasty piglet or two.

But in the end
It all got too much –
All that huffing and puffing
Up and down the den,
Muttering in his sleep
That he would blow the house down!

Something was wrong,
I could tell –
Something had put his nose
Out of joint.

He'd come home full of bravado,
Swaggering into the den,
Flashing me that wolfish grin –
All teeth and tongue –
Then he'd set about boasting,
Full of big talk about
blowing up another building.
It cut no ice with me.

The tell-tale signs were there –
Some days he'd get back
covered in straw,
hardly able to draw breath.
What he'd been up to,
Lord alone knows . . .

Well it all came to a head,
When late one afternoon
He shot back in,
With his fur singed.

I had to laugh –
He looked so funny,
Stood there with his bare bottom
Red as a radish.
Talk about coming home
With his tail between his legs!
Where he'd been – I can't imagine.
He never said.

He stays more at home now.
Well, he's prone to bronchitis –
This time of year
you can hear him coming,
Poor old thing –
Wheezing and puffing,
Hardly able to draw breath.

We don't talk about it –
And he's right off pork!
If you ask me,
It's all been
a bit of a blow
To his ego.

Pie Corbett

INTERVIEWS

Interviewing children in role is an excellent strategy for delving into a character's mind, motives and feelings. There is no pre-planning required – children sit in the 'hot seat' and take on the role of a character from a storybook or fairy tale, e.g. the woodcutter who saw Red walking towards Granny's house.

You might also use interviews in a more creative and imaginative way. How about interviewing Granny about her forthcoming role in a Steven Spielberg film – her life and ambitions? Or, maybe, interview Ron Weasley about his future life as a Quidditch world champion, or the hobbit Bilbo Baggins about his journey, his freelance life as a burglar on hire to dwarves seeking lost treasure.

WORKING AS JOURNALISTS

This game sees the children working in role as journalists and as characters from a story. To carry out the game successfully, they have to gather clues from the story about what has happened and move into role. It exercises oral skills such as questioning, explaining and describing. Children love it because it imitates a medium with which they are familiar – the TV!

Put children into small groups to work as journalists. They could prepare questions and interview a panel of characters from storybooks they've read. They could present 'the Six O'clock News' – complete with an outside broadcast, interviewing characters in the midst of the story. For instance, this might involve interviewing Ron and Hermione about recent events at Hogwarts, or the soldiers and Tim, the ostler, after the Highwayman's death.

DEBATES AND TRIALS

When stories have a major dilemma at their heart or characters who are faced with big decisions, they can be a valuable source for debates. Should 'The Iron Man' be destroyed? Should the Trunchbull be employed as Head teacher in our school?

An even more engaging idea is to take a dodgy character and put them on trial. For instance, the Wolf from *The Three Little Pigs* could be arrested and face trial. What about putting Boggis, Bunce and Bean on trial for attempted murder of foxes? Would there be a defence? After all, the fox does steal from them . . .

IF ONLY THE MIRROR COULD SPEAK

This is an interesting game which demands that the children have thought carefully about what has happened in a story. In a way, it is a form of comprehension! It involves digging under the skin of a character's motives, thoughts and feelings. It helps the children to stand outside of a text almost like an observer and begin to think about and comment on what is happening. Children enjoy the game because it involves a dramatic element.

- To play this game you need to start reading a story together as a class and then stop at an interesting moment.
- A group of four children sit in a square, facing inwards. Each member of the group is a mirror on the wall of a room.
- One at a time you choose other members of the class to walk into the square, introducing themselves as a character from the story.

- Remind the children of what was happening in the story when you stopped reading it. Tell them that you are now in a frozen moment when time has stopped and that you now have an opportunity to take a closer look at what is happening.
- The four children who are playing the mirrors take it in turns to talk about what is going on in the story. This could involve:
  - giving advice to the character standing in front of them
  - saying what might happen next
  - speaking the character's thoughts
  - commenting on what has happened.
- Each mirror could adopt a different stance, e.g. one might be sympathetic while another acts like a disapproving aunt.

ROLL ON STORY!

You will need: dice (enough for one between two), exercise books.

The random nature of this game means that all sorts of unlikely possibilities can be thrown up. This often triggers a new story idea rather than regurgitating something already written. The dice-rolling element appeals to children's love of games, and especially to those reading fighting fantasy books or who play Warhammer games.

- In this game children (in pairs) are given a selection of characters (goodies and baddies), feelings, opening settings, and main action locations (six of each) and use a dice to choose one from each of them. They use the information to plan a story which they then tell to their partner.

- Start by writing the following six headings on the whole-class board:
  - Goodies
  - Baddies
  - How the goody feels
  - How the baddy feels
  - Where the story starts
  - Where the action takes place
- Write down six examples under each heading, numbering them 1 to 6. An example has been provided for you below. (An interesting alternative is to let the children write their own list of goodies and baddies – the results can be spectacular!)

Goodies
1. Prince
2. Princess
3. Farmer
4. Woodcutter
5. Dog
6. Cat

Baddies
1. Dragon
2. Wolf
3. Giant
4. Goblin
5. Queen
6. King

How the goody feels
1. Clever
2. Excited
3. Adventurous
4. Brave
5. Strong
6. Kind

How the baddy feels
1. Cruel
2. Greedy
3. Spiteful
4. Jealous
5. Bad tempered
6. Mean

Where the story starts
1. Cottage
2. Market place
3. Pool
4. Hillside
5. City street
6. Farmyard

Where the action takes place
1. Tower
2. Dungeon
3. Crumbling bridge
4. Cave
5. Forest
6. Lonely path

- Taking a category at a time, the children roll their dice and look to see which element corresponds with the number they've rolled, e.g. if they were choosing a goody and they rolled a five, their hero would be a dog. If they then moved onto choosing a baddy and rolled a three, the villain of their tale would be a giant. Ask them to list the components of their story in their exercise books.
- When they have rolled the dice six times and listed the elements, the children should plan their story. Since they will be telling their story aloud to their partner, encourage them to jot down some notes that will act as a memory-jogger when the time comes to relate their story.
- Once the children have heard their partner's story and told their own, see if any of them want to share their tales with the whole class. Obviously, this method of generating a story can lead from telling into writing.

FREEZE FRAME

This is a set of games to use at interesting moments in a class story. To play the games the children have to have listened carefully to the story and think about how characters are feeling, their motives and what might happen next. The games encourage the children to empathise with others' emotions and situations. The games also contain an element of discussion that centres around social and moral dilemmas with a chance to share opinions and work out problems together.

The story spy
1.   Stop at an interesting moment in a story.
2.   Working in pairs, one child is a spy who has been 'eavesdropping' on what has just happened. The eavesdropper tells their partner (a friend) the gossip. They can both then decide what to do.

Role swaps
1.   Stop at an interesting moment in a story.
2.   Working in pairs, one child is in role as a main character in the story. They are telling their partner (a friend) about what is happening, and explaining how they feel. The friend is very sympathetic.
3.   After a few minutes signal to the children to swap roles.

Agony aunt
1.   Stop at an interesting moment in a story.
2.   Working in pairs, one child is a character in difficulty – perhaps with a choice to make about what to do – or maybe who is behaving foolishly. The other is an 'agony aunt'. The main character is visiting the agony aunt to

talk about what is going on. The aunt has to offer advice.

Rumours

1. Stop at an interesting moment in a story.
2. Working in pairs, one child is in role as a character from the story. The other spreads a rumour about another character. This might be true or false. The character either is taken in by the rumour and can move on to elaborate and spread the rumour further, or argues against the rumour, explaining what actually happened.

Phone a friend

This game is excellent for putting children in a position where they have to summarise what has happened in a story, discuss the plot and predict what will happen next. It is an active, comprehension activity that helps children enter the world of the story imaginatively.

1. Sit the children in pairs, back to back.
2. They get out their mobile phones (pretend) and one phones the other.
3. They talk – this is excellent if one is in role as a character from a book, telling the other about what has just happened, e.g. Red phoning home from Granny's house. Alternatively, they could be given a scenario, e.g. they have just witnessed a robbery.

PIP, SQUEAK AND WILFRED

This is guaranteed to give your class a great physical warm-up. It's a fast-moving activity designed to raise energy levels, and is a real favourite with children. You'll need as much room as possible to play it in – the hall or playground is best.

- Stand with the children in a circle. One child is chosen to be Pip and another is selected as Squeak.
- When you shout 'GO!' Pip runs round the outside of the circle in one direction and Squeak runs round in the opposite direction. After a few seconds you call out 'Home' and they both have to return to where they were originally standing as quickly as possible without changing direction.
- Once the children have got the hang of the game, introduce a third person as Wilfred. Wilfred has the advantage of being able to run randomly in either direction. Play the game again and see whether this makes a difference!

CROSSING THE BORDER

You will need: a chair, a blindfold (e.g. a scarf or similar piece of material).

This game is very handy for settling a class and helping them to listen carefully. To play this you will need total silence and concentration. It makes an excellent warm-up to drama or maybe a session on suspense writing.

- Sit everyone down at the side of the hall. Blindfold a volunteer who will act as the guard,

and guide the child over to the middle of the room.
- Select another who starts to walk from one end of the hall and has to cross the imaginary 'border', which the first child is guarding, to a fixed point at the other end of the hall (e.g. a chair).
- The guard moves from side to side and tries to capture the other child by touching them. Everyone else has to keep really quiet – they mustn't give the game away to the guard!
- If anyone manages to 'cross the border', they take over the role as guard.

ACT A HAT

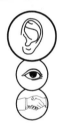

You will need: as wide a selection of hats as possible (e.g. top hat, flat cap, rain hat, cycle helmet, baseball cap, etc.)

This is an excellent jumpstart to working on characterisation in narrative. Children are invited to put on a hat and then speak in the role indicated by the type of hat they have chosen. The same game works well with other items of clothing (e.g. a cloak or shawl, a pair of shoes, a tie, etc.) or selected props (e.g. an umbrella, a handkerchief, a diary, etc.).

- Bring in a selection of hats and lay them out on a table. One at a time the children come forward and put on one of the hats.
- They then have a minute or two to talk in the manner they think that character would talk. You might need to provide a scenario to start the child off, e.g. the character has to walk into a shop and buy a pint of milk.

SWAP!

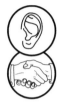

In this small group activity, children act and speak in character and after a short time swap roles with their partners. This gives them the chance to experience different perspectives and to see both sides of an argument.

- Choose two or three children to improvise a role, e.g. Mum and Dad are watching telly. Their child arrives back home late.
- Explain to the class that you will shortly be pressing the 'freeze-frame button', at which point they must freeze and swap roles with one of their partners.
- After a short while call out 'freeze' – the actors freeze and swap roles. On the words 'action' they start again, picking up from where the scene left off, but in a different role.

TRIANGLE SCENES

This is a really good game for getting ideas flowing and for strengthening the imagination. It is based on a form of brainstorming, and involves setting and improvising a scene. This makes an interesting precursor to writing and emphasises an important point about story writing – if you don't know what to do next, introduce something new to shift the plot in a different direction!

- Pick out three people. They sit in a triangle. Point to each in turn. The first has to choose a setting, 'We are in a wood'. The second decides on a scenario, e.g. an alien has just found a dog. The third chooses the three characters they will play, e.g. the alien, the dog and a policeman.

- Now they improvise the scene. Everyone else sits round in a circle – goldfish bowl style.
- Bring characters in and out. Freeze action if the children stumble or the pace drags. Ask the class to suggest how the action could be moved forwards. This may be by introducing something new – a phone call, letter, new character, or a sudden turn of events.

BEAT THIS!

This idea works in a similar way to the 'Boasting' game (p. 74) as the children pass ideas backwards and forwards, constantly trying to outdo each other. It takes some skill if it is to work well as they have to gradually build up their ideas.

- Divide the class into pairs. The first child says something fairly mundane, e.g. 'I've found £5'. Their partner takes the idea but exaggerates it, e.g. 'I've found a nugget of gold', and always adds 'but don't tell anyone' onto the end of the sentence, e.g.

> *Child 1:* I've found £5.
> *Child 2:* I've found a nugget of gold, but don't tell anyone.
> *Child 1:* I've found a gold bar, but don't tell anyone.
> *Child 2:* I've found a sack of diamonds, but don't tell anyone.
> *Child 1:* I've found a chest of priceless treasure, but don't tell anyone.

- The exaggerations can pass back and forwards, gradually outdoing each other. It works well if the couple build up the exaggerations bit by bit.

RESET IT

This activity is ideal as a warm-up to a writing session where you intend to talk about different genres. Before playing the game it might be handy to write a list of different genres on the whole-class board, e.g. mystery, detective, sci-fi, fantasy, school, ghost, etc. Under these brainstorm stock characters, settings and events. This information will be handy when playing the game.

- Select a setting, e.g. in an office. Have two or three characters improvising a short scene. You may need to provide a prompt to the action, e.g. a phone call comes through to say that the business is going to be sold and they might lose their jobs.
- The scene is enacted for a short while, e.g. a minute or two. Then it has to be re-enacted as if it was in a different genre, e.g. a children's comedy, a soap, a sci-fi film, a horror story, etc.
- At the end of the game, return to the brainstorm and add any ideas that arose during the drama. It may be useful, for instance, to write down any typical words or phrases that were used, gestures, etc. It is also worth discussing which genre was the easiest to work with and why.

GOOD NEWS/BAD NEWS

This is a game that the whole class play together. Not only will it reinforce children's turn-taking skills, but it is also a great way to encourage the children to concentrate and listen. It also lends itself to an element of 'wit' which always goes down well!

Start the game off with a piece of good news, e.g. 'The good news is that tomorrow is a holiday for the school'. Then choose a child to offer a piece of bad news, e.g. 'The bad news is that you have been selected to help clean up the playground'. To keep children on their toes, select randomly whose turn it is next. They alternate with good news and bad news, e.g.

Teacher:	The good news is that tomorrow is a holiday for the school.
Child 1:	The bad news is that you have been selected to help clean up the playground.
Child 2:	The good news is that there will be a free lunch.
Child 3:	The bad news is that it consists of onions.
Child 4:	The good news is that the onions are sprinkled on a pizza . . .

COME WITH ME

This is another simple yet effective game which encourages youngsters to listen attentively to one another. The aim of the activity is for children to guess what type of character a volunteer is playing (e.g. bossy, shy, miserable, etc.) by listening to a few words spoken by the child. It would make a handy warm-up for any session where you are looking at characterisation – in reading or writing.

Children take it in turns to say 'come with me' in different ways. Others have to guess the character type – bossy, shy, aggressive, miserable, lonely, etc. or job, e.g. ballet dancer, teacher, soldier, doctor, etc. It may be worth pausing the children and discussing the need for clarity as well as expression when speaking – especially when performing. Tease away at the use of facial expression and gestures to add emphasis and character. The children should think about how these can be added to writing, e.g. *his face twisted as he spat out the words* . . .

WINK

This is an old favourite that children love to play. It makes a great drama warm-up as it requires concentration and participation from the whole group. Children adore the secret element.

- The class sit in a circle and you choose a 'detective'. This person is sent out of the room.
- Everyone else closes their eyes and you tap one of them on the back. This person is the 'murderer'.
- The 'detective' re-enters the room and sits in the centre of the circle. Everyone looks at each other. The 'murderer' has to wink or blink at the other children to 'kill' them without being seen by the 'detective'.
- The 'murdered' child leans forward and plays dead until a new game starts. The 'detective' can challenge the 'murderer' if they think they know who it is. If they guess incorrectly three times, a new game begins.
- You could add a further dimension to the game by letting the children 'die' more dramatically, or by choosing more than one 'detective' and/or 'murderer'.

NURSERY RHYMES AND FAIRY TALES

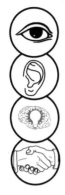

You may find that you have to begin this series of jumpstarts by reminding the children of some well-known nursery rhymes and fairy tales. The beauty of these is that there is such a rich variety to choose from. They can be used as the basis for all sorts of different activities that never fail to get the brain buzzing!

Rhymes and stories are brought to life in the games below, with the help of dramatic techniques such as hot seating, role-play, improvisation, etc. Enjoy!

Hot seating

Take a character from a nursery rhyme and 'hot seat' them, e.g. put Humpty Dumpty on a chair and question him as a class:

> Why were you sitting on the wall?
> Were you pushed or did you fall?
> Did you notice anyone looking suspicious before you were pushed?
> Why did you disobey your mother's warning about sitting on the town wall?

Whoever is chosen to sit in the 'hot seat' must answer as their character would.

Guess who?

Someone role-plays a character from a nursery rhyme or fairy tale and the class have ten questions to find out who they are. The children will need to think hard about what questions are most likely to help them guess who the mystery character is.

Retell

This is a real brain-teaser which is harder than you might think! The children have to retell/rewrite a well-known rhyme without using the letter 'e', e.g.

> Jack and Jill ran up a hill
> to buy a spot of nosh;
> hitting a patch of oil, poor Jack
> took flight and spilt his squash.

Thoughts in the head

Someone walks up to the front of the class and pretends they are the main character in a nursery rhyme or fairy tale. They retell what happened using the first person, as if they were gossiping after the event. You might like to start them off by taking on the role of a character yourself, e.g.

> My name's Cinderella and I've just come back up to my room after a wonderful night at the ball, where I was the guest of honour! (I can't wait to get these shoes off – I've been on my feet all night.) I haven't always lived in a palace you know – I've had it rough over the years. I used to live with my evil stepmother and ugly sisters who bossed me about and treated me like a slave.

> That was until my Fairy Godmother appeared and changed my life! She lent me a lovely dress and glass slippers, and a carriage to take me to a ball that the charming Prince was holding. When the magic ran out at Midnight and I had to leave the ball in a hurry, he found my slipper and didn't stop until he had tracked me down. It was so romantic! And when the slipper fit, no-one could believe it! Even in my rags, the Prince said I was his princess. Somehow, I don't think anyone will be calling me Cinders again.

Storyboard
Draw a simple storyboard on the whole-class board showing the key events in a nursery rhyme or fairy tale. These can then be used for retelling it. A refashioned *Jack and the Beanstalk* might look something like this:

1. Jack leaving home, leading cow.
2. Jack being given magic bean.
3. Plants bean in window-box.
4. Jack climbs bean through clouds.
5. Emerges onto a sunny beach.
6. Dons sunglasses, licks ice-cream.
7. Stands on rocks talking to mermaid.
8. Gets her an ice-cream.
9. She gives him a large shell.
10. Climbs back down with shell.
11. Explains to mother – if you put your ear to shell you can hear the future . . .

CHAPTER 6
Jumpstarting learning

Over the last few years teachers have become increasingly interested in discovering strategies for helping children become better learners. These games are intended to gain full participation and attention right from the start of a lesson. They are handy for developing listening and concentration as well as engaging children in thinking. I see these games as a kind of 'mental gymnastics' that can be used to warm up the brain so that children are engaged, their brains buzzing and eager to work. Of course, the games are not exclusive to literacy and could be used in any subject to tune the children into learning.

WHAT I KNOW OR WISH I KNEW!

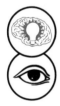

A sure-fire way to get a topic underway is to pool as much information as you can on what children already know and to find out what they'd like to learn more about.

- Brainstorm together as a class, listing things the children know about the chosen topic on the whole-class board.
- Next tap into children's natural curiosity by encouraging them to suggest things they would like to find out about. They should write these down on paper and keep the list safe. At the end of a unit of work they should revisit this list and note down what they did find out, what is still waiting to be explored, plus any unexpected things they discovered.

MEMORY LISTS

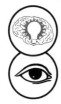

Memory lists are an excellent way to tune children back into a topic and to make links with the previous sessions.

- Ask children to rapidly list on their mini-whiteboards what they recall about a topic you have already covered. For instance, say you are revisiting 'Life cycles' with the group – the children could be asked to write down three things about the topic. These might include:
  - what they learned
  - what they found most interesting
  - what surprised them most
  - whether they have found out anything new about the subject since you looked at it together.

- As an extension to this activity, see if the children can make a list of the most amazing things they have learnt about a unit of work. They can do this on their mini-whiteboards, or present them as posters.

MIND MAPS

These can be used to generate ideas and to help children organise their thinking. When someone has lots of ideas buzzing around in their head, it often helps if they get them down on paper in a clear and memorable form. That way they can start to see patterns and links, which in turn generates more ideas.

- Before the children make mind maps of their own, do a whole-class example to show them how it's done. For instance, this could be used as a strategy for generating ideas for a story or organising thoughts about how to improve your school. Whatever the topic is, write the heading of the topic in the centre of the whole-class board.

- From there, draw lines outwards and write down the main ideas or headings that relate to the topic. Under these, gather relevant notes. A simple mind map might look something like this:

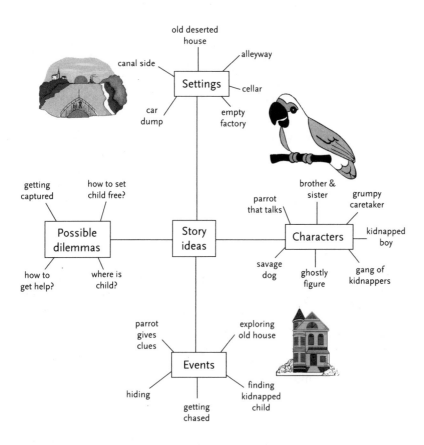

DRAW IT

Much information becomes more memorable if it is drawn rather than written down. This approach is especially useful for those who struggle to remember facts, e.g. scientific concepts such as how reflections are caused. It's a particularly useful technique for visual learners. Try it and see!

Reflections are caused by light bouncing off things. When this light is reflected into our eyes, we are able to see things.

BREAK IT DOWN

A great way to get to grips with a topic or unit of work is to break it down into smaller parts. The same is true for diagrams, pictures or texts. Faced with a complicated picture or piece of text, the best thing to do is to pull it apart bit by bit.

Photocopy pictures or texts for children to interrogate. They could circle things they are unsure of, highlight the most important points, insert statements or questions in different colours and so on.

BEAT THE EXPERTS

A fun way to see how much information children have retained after a unit of work is to play 'Beat the experts'. This is in the form of a question-and-answer session and it involves children quizzing a panel of experts (four or five of their classmates) to see how much they've learnt. Try to keep the whole thing light-hearted and fun!

- Divide the class into groups of four or five. One of the groups sits at the front of the class as the panel of experts.
- One by one their classmates ask them questions on the topic just covered. Points should be awarded for each correct answer (ask for a volunteer to keep score).
- Once the panel has been asked 10–15 questions, they are replaced with a new set of panellists. When every group has taken their turn as experts count up the scores and see who the winners are!
- An alternative quiz game to play at the end of a unit of work is based on the hit TV programme 'Who Wants to be a Millionaire?' One child sits in the 'hot seat' and is asked a series of questions, each one becoming increasingly difficult. The other children act as the audience and the usual rules apply, i.e. the volunteer has three lifelines – phone a friend, ask the audience and 50/50 (determined by the chief questioner – the teacher!).

TRUE OR FALSE?

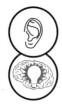

We spoke earlier about how fascinated children are with lying and how many of them perfect the art of 'bending the truth'! This activity is an ideal opportunity to put this faculty to good use, and allows you to see how many facts they have remembered.

- The children take it in turns to produce a 'true or false' statement for the topic they're revising, e.g. 'The Romans ate hamsters – true or false?'
- Pick someone to say whether this is true or false (of course, it's false in this instance – the Romans ate stuffed dormice!).
- An extension of this activity is to ask each child to present three facts and one lie about the topic, e.g.

    1. The Romans were very religious and worshipped many gods.
    2. Romans spoke Italian.
    3. The Romans invented camouflage – their navy wore blue to match the sea.

Can the other children spot the lie?

WHAT THE PAPERS SAY

Here are three entertaining activities that are designed to follow initial work on a topic. In the first two, the children act as journalists, inventing headlines and advertisements based on the topic they are studying. The third sees the class being interviewed by a panel of interested aliens!

Headlines

The class invent headlines for important pieces of information. This links particularly well with history, geography, science and religion. Use it to see if children can recall important features of what's been heard. Example headlines might include:

HEATWAVE HALTS WORK ON GREAT PYRAMID

BEAM OF LIGHT BENDS UNDER WATER

MIRACLE CURE – LAZARUS LIVES

Advertise facts

The children write 'For sale' notices or adverts for characters from history, or facts they've learnt, e.g.

For sale
One old King. Has had 5 wives
though careless on occasions.
Plays music, sings and writes poetry . . .

Alien interview

This may sound a bit out of the ordinary, but it's an activity that has proved to be very popular with youngsters. A panel of investigative alien journalists has been sent to interview the children about the topic they have been studying. The aliens aren't familiar with earthly ways and need help to make sense of the topic so that they can write a column for their paper, *The Planet*. Give the 'aliens' a few moments to think of some questions.

MUSIC

Many teachers play gentle, classical music to their class to encourage a relaxed yet focused mood for working. Research has shown that classical music is processed in the same part of the brain that also develops language and mathematics. There is now a body of research which suggests that certain music stimulates abstract reasoning, mathematical thinking, spatial awareness as well as creativity and motivation. Mozart is considered to be the most effective.

Naxos sell a double CD of Mozart specifically with this in mind, titled 'Listen, Learn and Grow with Mozart'. You should be able to order this through any CD store or get a catalogue from 'Select Music and Video Distribution Ltd, 34 Holmethorpe Avenue, Redhill, Surrey RH1 2NN. One CD is for 'movement, fun and play' and the other is for 'contemplation, rest and relaxation'. I use either side when I'm working or writing creatively and it certainly seems to make my thinking clearer. I can almost feel my mind tingling with ideas. Obviously this would prove useful for mathematics, creative activities and stimulating the mind.

Try playing something soothing like Mahler to create a restful mood when you're trying to calm children down and settle them to work. It might also be worth experimenting with other composers such as Haydn.

Another way to use music is right at the start of a session to get control, deepen concentration and encourage full participation. Use a rain stick or hit a cymbal to focus listening – 'Who can hear the moment when the sound of the cymbal fades?' The idea is that everyone sits silently, straining to hear the last echo of the note fading away. By then you should have total silence and concentration!

ACTION!

Play a game such as 'Simon Says' to generate physical movement and get the mind working and concentrating. Throw in a few difficult moves such as rubbing the tummy and patting the head at the same time, or crossing from the left knee to the right shoulder with the same hand (or vice versa).

MIME IT

Children love pretending. This activity is an unusual strategy that children really enjoy. It involves a lot of thinking as well as miming! Mime is simply moving without speaking. If you have played charades with your class, they will be familiar with the idea.

In pairs, children take it in turns to mime something they learnt in a previous session. Their partner tries to guess who they are or what they are doing, then they swap over. The children should pick an action that people, animals or things do, e.g. a chrysalis opening to reveal a butterfly, a slave building a Roman road and so on. Alternatively, they could choose a character from the past if the focus is historical, e.g. the Pharaoh, a Roman Centurion, etc.

GOSSIP

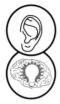

This is a quick and easy verbal activity that can be used at the end of a unit of teaching to reinforce learning. Gossip is a simple and effective device for exploring what's just been learnt.

In pairs, the children stand and imagine there is a fence between them and their partner. Pretending to lean on the fence, they gossip about what they have learnt in the last unit of work. They could talk about knowledge gained, skills developed, or their thoughts about how they set about learning.

DID YOU KNOW?

This works in much the same way as the 'Gossip' activity above and is a great way to round off a unit of work.

- Working in pairs, the children take it in turns to discuss a topic. Their conversation should follow this sort of format:

    Did you know that . . .
    Yes, and I also knew that . . .

- But there's a snag! Every so often they should try to catch their partner out by slipping in a lie. The children will have to listen closely and think about what they've learnt if they're going to spot these red herrings.